THINK AGAIN'S
QUEER YOUTH MANIFESTO

1. The right to my history and to learn about lesbians, gays, transgenders & bisexuals as part of my basic education.

2. The right to ask for support without fear from friends, family, employers and teachers.

3. The right to choose partners and friends without feeling shame.

4. The right to feel safe from violence or prejudice at home, school and work.

5. The right to community and to mentors & role models at school & in my neighborhood.

6. The right to explore my body and to decide when, where and with whom I experiment sexually.

7. The right to my ethnic and racial identity and to refuse to choose between my sexual identity and my heritage.

8. The right to information about my body, including accurate information about becoming sexual, sexually transmitted diseases and pregnancy.

9. The right to be seen as a whole person and to reject stereotypes which define me only in terms of sex.

10. The right to respect.

IN 1998, THE U.S. REVOKED THE RIGHTS OF IMMIGRANTS, REVOKED WELFARE, AND KICKED ONE MILLION CHILDREN INTO POVERTY. IN THE SAME YEAR, THE WEALTHIEST 10% OF AMERICANS OWNED OVER 70% OF THE NATION'S WEALTH.

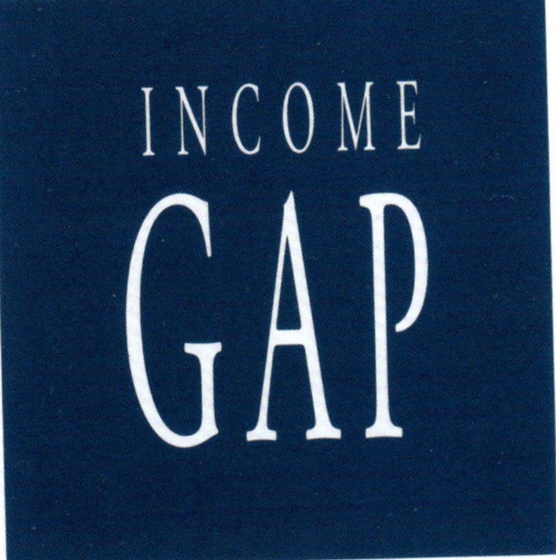

11. The right to speak out.

THINK AGAIN are artists who strike back at mainstream and wheat-paste can still incite people to THINK

America, land of the free-with-purchase.

THINK AGAIN are artists who strike back at mainstream and wheat-paste can still incite people to THINK

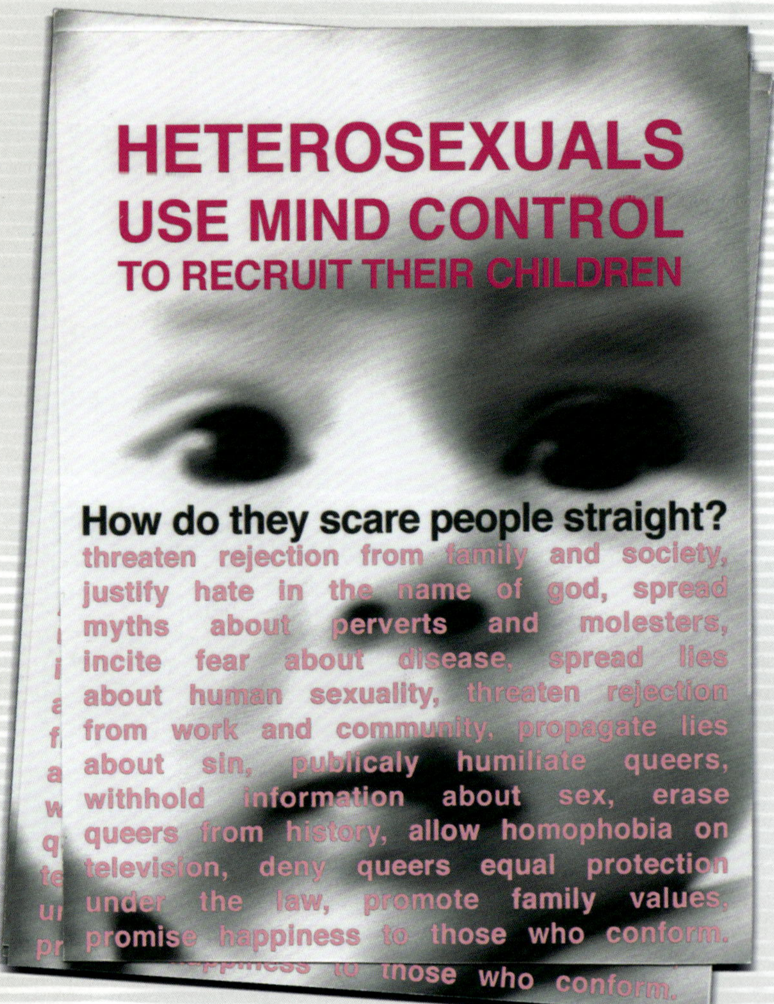

A BRIEF HISTORY OF OUTRAGE

THINK AGAIN expects something political from art. We use images to challenge mainstream ideas that perpetuate injustice.

THINK AGAIN recruits artmaking in the service of political action. As an artist-activist collaborative, we design and distribute graphic materials, produce media campaigns, stage street actions, and hand out agitprop at community events. Our work combines grassroots politics, cultural theory, sociological evidence, and humor to create a visual language for talking about public life. We've taken on an array of progressive political issues from race justice to the structural violence against women and from hate crimes to the meat industrial complex. We use Xerox machines and wheat-paste to prompt people to THINK AGAIN.

We distribute much of our work in face-to-face encounters with people on the street and use agitprop to spark conversations. Some people stop and react to the work for a few moments; others join us in a discussion for an hour. We are energized when people engage ideas about why welfare was revoked or whether a pre-emptive attack is justified. In every interaction we try to understand what fuels cultural backlash and how people develop their sense of collective justice, humanity, and democracy. These encounters force THINK AGAIN to reconsider what constitutes the political mainstream, what kind of power it has, and how the Right effectively obscures ideological and economic injustice.

THINK AGAIN is sad to report that many of these conversations make us wonder if producing political indifference is one of the monumental accomplishments of contemporary culture in the United States. What kind of society condones blithely stepping over a homeless person in a city street and ignoring a complaint of hunger, while holding a blended coffee that costs more than half the minimum hourly wage?

THINK AGAIN wonders whether the sheer speed of culture creates ethical vertigo such that what appears to be indifference is actually confusion. Most of us don't blink as our eyes shift from front-page stories about ethnic cleansing to busses shrink-wrapped with Citibank advertisements. We process loss, environmental devastation, self-actualization, and greed within a short segment of a primetime drama. Mediated images tinker with perceptions of control as wage laborers try to find affordable daycare and unravel embedded reports on weapons of mass destruction. THINK AGAIN reluctantly plays along – we interrupt this speed and challenge pedestrians to distinguish between agitprop and HBO ads.

However, attributing indifference to speed alone is too convenient. So THINK AGAIN questions the social institutions that invest monstrous amounts of creativity and capital to guarantee that people are sufficiently mystified and politically stymied. The purveyors of propaganda – from ad agencies to the Pentagon – hire teams of graphic artists, purchase ad space, secure product placements, and plaster advertisements on everything. The Pentagon has a dedicated line item for this activity. Perhaps the purveyors coax the society's unapologetic fascination with its own economic and military privilege. Does a market pre-exist for oxymoronic fetishes like luxury tanks, camouflage lingerie, and homeless-chic fashions?

THINK AGAIN's impulse to plaster political posters on the city streets is a desire to convert consumers into environmentalists, gays into queers, carnivores into vegetarians, television executives into human rights advocates. It's a desire to make a democracy act like a democracy.

We have worked hard to generate art about these issues with minimal indictment, since we too are implicated in the structures that produce all sorts of racist, sexist, and globalized human suffering. By and large, if you are reading this you have eaten junk food, purchased a pair of sweatshop jeans, fantasized about an overpaid movie star, paid taxes to a war machine, and speak the language most associated with colonial and post-colonial enterprises.

Unfortunately, feeling implicated and without agency tends to amplify indifference and justify inaction. Certainly the status quo benefits when politically progressive people yawn the postmodern yawn and talk fatalistically about racism or empire as totalizing, impenetrable, and irresistible. (Though Miami-Dade's unresolved chads and Halliburton's newest contract hardly make the case for participatory government.)

THINK AGAIN finds it challenging to make agitprop that treads the line between critique and action. On the one hand, we focus on how structures of power are linked to and produce experience. We make connections between cherishing a wedding ring and international labor (*Popping the Question,* 1999) or rape and NAFTA (*Hello/Hola,* 2002). On the other hand, we make work that taps into people's individual sense of political possibility, gives permission to have an opinion or to resist, and moves beyond sloganeering or consciousness-raising to local political action.

THINK AGAIN revels in the moment of rupture and awareness when a teenage girl looks down at a plate of bacon and pictures the hog. These moments of political imagination challenge

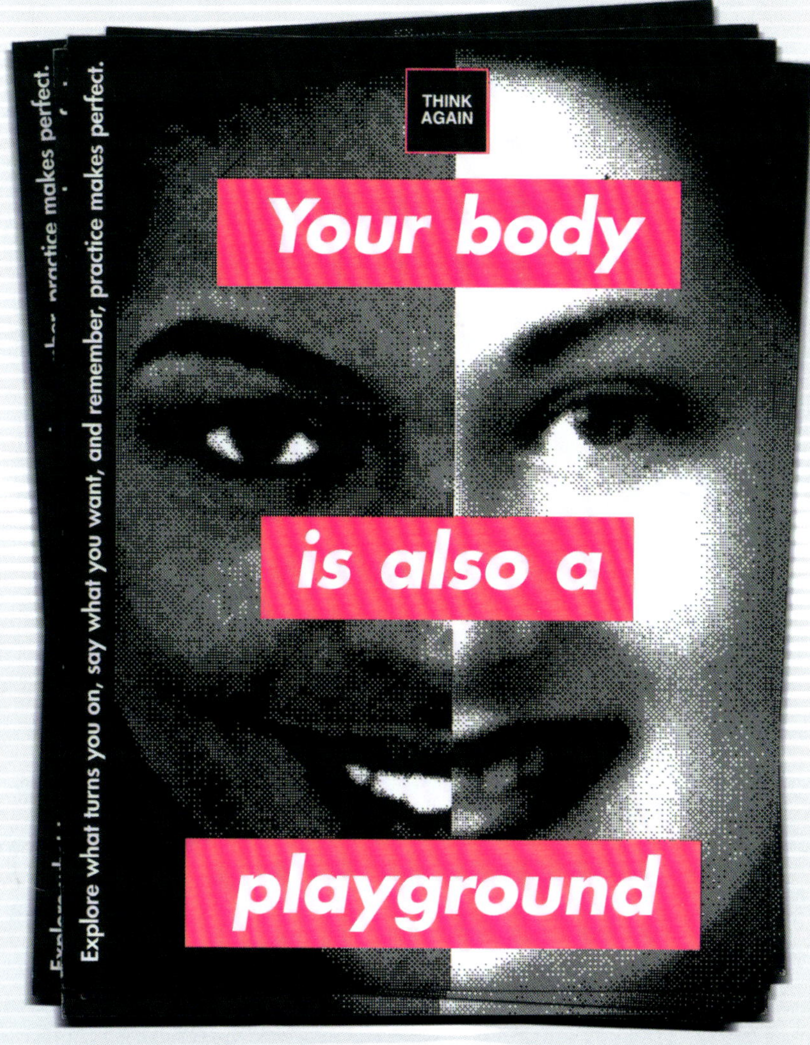

efforts by consumerist culture, mainstream media, and "patriots" to obscure our sight from the real conditions of violence, labor, and suffering.

THINK AGAIN draws inspiration from late eighties activism when artists effectively helped society imagine social transformation and mobilize political action. There is a long list of precedents; we are influenced by collaboratives like Gran Fury, Group Material, and the Lesbian Avengers. And like some of these collectives, the starting point for THINK AGAIN emerges from our interest in problems facing queers. Most importantly, we argue that there are no issues facing queers that are neutral in regard to racism, sexism, or economics.

As a strategy for shifting away from the identity politics of the nineties and returning to an activism based on social transformation, we use queer as a conceptual touchstone in our work. We see homophobia as a set of cultural myths about sex and bodies that masquerade as truths about human nature. A queer criticality compels us to dismantle propagandist stories across issues. THINK AGAIN attempts to redress myths about uncivilized Arabs, irresponsible welfare queens, lazy homeless people, and fears of anyone black or brown. It is not surprising that these subjects sit at the center of society's moral panic, with brown people, poor people, and queer people always threatening to unravel the social fabric.

THINK AGAIN also converses extensively and collaborates with people doing the difficult work of mobilizing communities, influencing policy, and fashioning concrete political goals. And like our allies, THINK AGAIN makes an effort to reconcile contemporary problems facing progressive and queer organizing efforts. On the one hand, we question progressive initiatives that focus primarily on economic justice, the global marketplace, and civil liberties, but systematically exclude a critique of the cultural logic of homophobia and racism. And although increasingly some non-queer organizations include sexual liberation in their missions, we fear that homophobia and racism become addenda to what these organizations see as the primary work of establishing, for example, limits to economic imperialism, local control over economies, fair labor practices, and multilateralism.

On the other hand, THINK AGAIN is concerned about the co-optation of the queer movement by gay assimilationists who argue that to gain concrete political victories GLBT leadership should use conventional political processes and appeal to corporate interests. This approach requires that queers remain (largely) silent on issues pertaining to class, race, sexual difference, and misogyny. It also requires that we abide by the same political and self-censorship that straight people do (i.e. insist everyone aspires to have a traditional family, refrain from talking explicitly about sex, and ignore anyone living below the poverty line).

While the culture contemplates why Will can't find a boyfriend at Grace's wedding reception, THINK AGAIN wonders what happened to curriculum reform, queer-affirmative labor laws, public condom distribution, inclusive sex education, GLBT teen suicide prevention, and broadened visibility for transgenders and bisexuals. We squirm as property ownership, wealth accumulation, marriage, and Pottery Barn sofas become the signs of desirable gay and lesbian lives.

Is it unreasonable to expect a progressive movement not confined by sexual prudishness and a "gay agenda" not driven by materialism? (For that matter, is it unreasonable to expect a queer movement not caught in sexual prudishness, one that views sexual desire as politically productive rather than politically suicidal?) THINK AGAIN expects all progressive movements to address the cultural structures of homophobia that will persist even after gay TV characters adopt children together or Congress approves a living wage.

But let's be practical, what can we realistically expect from a work of political art?

Although implementing cross-issue politics is daunting in practice, it may be easier to design for offset press. THINK AGAIN conceives of projects that support a vision of politics against fragmentation and encourage alliances across communities. This requires designing agitprop that offers multiple points of entry and acknowledges the unequal effects of power on different cultural groups. For example, *Queer Essentials* – a series of sixteen postcards that first appeared in 1998 – is a collection of comments on domestic policies and political debates during the Clinton years. Commentary on hate crimes, the revoking of immigrant rights, and preliminary challenges to affirmative action appeared in a single pack and were distributed at an array of issue-oriented community events across the country.

THINK AGAIN sees imagemaking as an accessible, flexible form of social critique as well as a mode of posing a question, making a counterpoint, and offering public information. Our political graphics are jam-packed with analysis. Operating between the sound bite and the editorial, we argue that "community revitalization" is a euphemism for displacement (*White Blight,* 1999) and that the rhetoric of humanitarian aid is a propagandist strategy (*Humanitarian Daily Ration,* 2001).

THINK AGAIN sees political art as an organizing tool and a method for igniting face-to-face conversations. All of the projects included in *A Brief History of Outrage* were distributed for free through community organizations, and via direct distribution and the internet. We hand out postcards at Pride parades, park mobile billboards in front of television studios (*CIA TV*, 2001), and send digital posters to nonprofits trying to mobilize against the war machine (*Protestgraphics*, 2003). In this process, we try to meet the broadest range of people from angry conservatives who throw the postcards in the trash to our allies who post them on the fridge or hang them in offices. It's all a form of political work. Additionally, much of THINK AGAIN's artwork is exhibited in museums and reprinted in magazines and books.

Creating agitprop that appears in public requires THINK AGAIN to confront the changing reality of what constitutes public space and how and by whom it is controlled. THINK AGAIN grapples with the increasing disappearance of physical space for agitprop, the proliferation of advertising on everything, the pervasive censorship by media companies, the surveillance of guerrilla interventions by law enforcement, and since 9/11, the increasing acceptance of federally produced propaganda.

A Brief History of Outrage presents a range of strategies aimed at undoing the corporatization and surveillance of public space. Our efforts exploit the contextual meaning of location. THINK AGAIN places artwork where social and economic classes intersect (e.g., billboards about gentrification appearing along commuter routes). We distribute work where people are just as likely to be straight or queer (e.g., handing out postcards about sodomy at a neighborhood restaurant). We intervene where people expect to be silenced or policed (e.g., billboards questioning state sanctioned marriage in front of City Hall). We glue where people expect to see the morning news (e.g., "headlines" about anti-militarism stickered over newspaper vending machines). We intercede where people go to consume (e.g., postcards surreptitiously slipped into "Go-Card" advertising racks, holiday cards inserted into greeting card boxes at Kmart).

Most of THINK AGAIN's work from 1997 to 2003 appears in this book, arranged thematically. *A Brief History of Outrage* includes artwork combining photography, design, digital imaging, drawing, and collage. Additionally, we provide photographic documentation of the work to illustrate how it appears in context. *A Brief History of Outrage* also includes a new series of collages, entitled *Samples #1-11*, which appear on pages opposite our work from the previous six years. Combining unaltered advertising images and documentary photographs, the collages mine the symbolic terrain of advertising and mass media and set these pub-lic languages against a radically different kind of imagery.

With the collages, we investigate how public images deploy explicit and implicit political content and structure the polity's conception of civic life. *Samples #1-11* also provide context to the topics that THINK AGAIN has considered; they draw from some of the most prominent images in our culture. For example, Target comments on gentrification, Altoids comments on hate crimes, and Fox TV comments on funding federal intelligence. Public images also capitalize on and manipulate private fantasies and fears, translating empire into lifestyle (Kenneth Cole), social work into bathroom tile (Ann Sacks), and conflict diamonds into intimacy (De Beers).

Of course, work that ignites a progressive political imagination must also contend with the opposing cultural institutions that try to encourage people to think and act conservatively, defend the status quo, and denigrate progressive politics. *Samples #1-11* expose how the mass media colludes in cultural backlash and how mediated images are enmeshed with the fabric of daily life. Finally, *Samples #1-11* reflect an aspect of our larger critical project over the past six years: one that investigates correspondences between lived experience and represented reality, fact and fiction, and political process and mystification.

It is the nature of mediated culture to invert the scale of things, to make Calvin ads the size of skyscrapers and to insist that wars are necessary inconveniences. It is through creative acts that consumer culture translates everything into a commodity or market. And it is via acts of imagination that the political machine exploits fear in the service of empire. We are outraged at the super-slick, MTV-styled Army promos that reconfigure enlisting in a war machine as an act of self-realization. The lights dim and the theater quiets as *An Army of One* screens before *Eight Mile* begins, Eminem appearing as himself.

THINK AGAIN dissents. *A Brief History of Outrage* attempts to restore things to size.

David John Attyah   S.A. Bachman

THINK AGAIN Projects, in order of appearance

Queer Essentials Issue: Cultural backlash during the Clinton years. **Action:** Postcard series handed out at community events and distributed to grassroots organizations, 1998-1999.

White Blight Issue: Gentrification, displacement, and the renewed fashionability of US central cities. **Action:** Posters wheat-pasted on luxury loft construction in San Francisco and Boston, 1999.

Economic Boom For Whom? Issue: The rhetoric of prosperity mystifies the widening wealth gap of the 1990's. **Action:** Four billboards along commuter routes in Jamaica Plain, Mattapan, Somerville, and Dorchester, MA, 1999. *In collaboration with United for a Fair Economy.*

No Bullshit Issue: Creation of a "displacement free zone" to stop the destruction of moderate and low income housing in Los Angeles' Figueroa Corridor. **Action:** Poster campaign, Los Angeles, 2002. *In collaboration with Strategic Actions for a Just Economy, Center for the Study of Political Graphics, and Self-Help Graphics.*

Hello/Hola Issue: Systemic political, cultural, and economic forces produce sexualized violence against women in Cuidad Juarez, Mexico. **Action:** Postcard campaign and installation, 2002.

Poverty Among Women Issue: Revoking of welfare. **Action:** Holiday cards distributed via direct mail; guerrilla action loading cards into gift boxes at retail stores, 1998.

Human Abuse of Animals Issue: Torture of animals in the meat industrial complex. **Action:** Holiday cards distributed via direct mail; guerrilla action loading cards into gift boxes at retail stores, 1999.

Popping The Question Issue: State sanctioned marriage confers economic benefits exclusively to couples. **Action:** Truck caravan of mobile billboards in San Francisco and Boston, 2000.

Target Marketing Is Not A Social Movement Issue: Are queers visible or merely commercially viable? **Action**: Guerrilla intervention in "Go Card" postcard advertising racks, 2001; mobile billboard at '02 Los Angeles Dyke March and Gay Pride.

Advertising Works Because You Don't Think It Does Issue: Culture of dissatisfaction. **Action:** Guerrilla intervention in "Go Card" postcard advertising racks, 2001.

Protestgraphics Issue: Unjust US military action in the Middle East and Central Asia, violence against Arab and Muslim Americans, and the Bush administration's "infinite war" on terrorism. **Action:** Graphic materials distributed via online web resource at www.protestgraphics.org; direct distribution at political events, 2001-2003.

CIA TV Issue: Is it a conflict of interest for federal intelligence agencies to collaborate with television networks? **Action:** Two mobile billboards in Los Angeles; classified ads in the *Hollywood Reporter* and *Variety* (not pictured); web debate at www.CIATV.net, 2001-2002.

Act Like It's A Globe, Not An Empire Issue: US military invasion of Iraq peddled as an alternative to multilateralism. **Action:** Headline glued over newspaper vending machines; wheat-paste posters along major avenues, Los Angeles, 2003.

Homophobia Is Not Hilarious Issue: Media representation does not equal political representation. **Action:** Postcard write-in campaign to television executives, 1999.

A Brief History of Outrage

Published by Politicizing Pictures Press
Book orders: outrage@agitart.org
and through D.A.P./Distributed Art Publishers: www.artbook.com
Book and cover design by THINK AGAIN
Printed in Iceland by Oddi Printing
THINK AGAIN: www.agitart.org

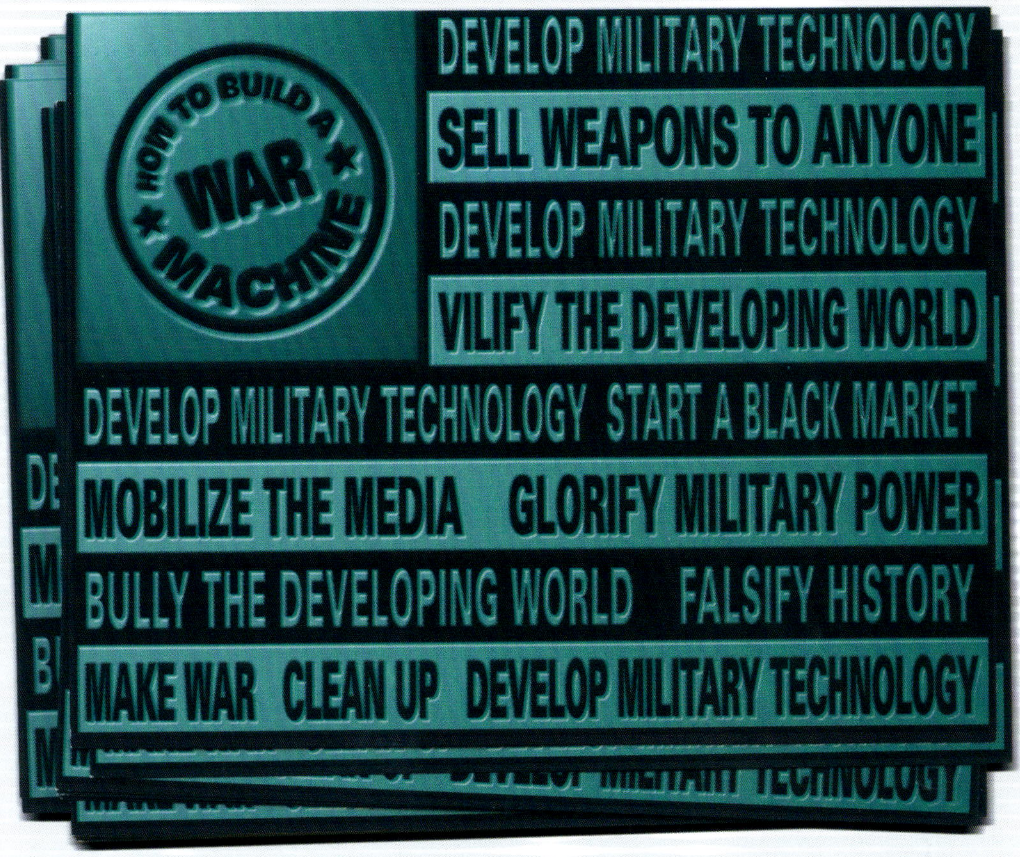

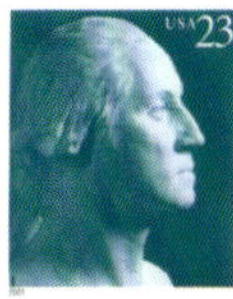

World military spending = $780 billion/year. That's roughly 19 times the cost to provide education, health care and nutrition to the entire world population.

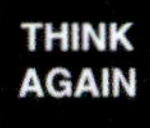

This book was supported by the LEF Foundation.

THINK AGAIN thanks:
Dunya Alwan • Marilyn Arsem
Gary Bachman • Judy Baca
Judie Bamber • Kelly Bennett
Max Berkelhammer • Jacquelyn C. Black
Laura Blacklow • Bill Burke
Magdalena Campos-Pons • David Clennon
Sue Coe • Bonnie Donohue • Jim Dow
Natalie Egnatchi • Lalla A. Essaydi
Steve Filandrinos • Greg Garvan
Jane Gillooly • jenn joy • Claudia Koonz
John Lapham • Jason Linetzky
Warren Longmire • Irene Meldon
Lazaro Montano • Hirokazu Miyazaki
David Mussina • Henri Myers
Robert M. Myers • Dang Ngo
Debra Padilla • Jan Paris • Dillon Paul
Deborah Ratner • Ron Ratner
Annelise Riles • Abe Rybeck
Amy Scholder • Larry Shea
Jeannie Simms • Laurel Sparks
Jose Lebrero Stals • Sandy Stark
Mary Ellen Strom • Amy Villarejo
Carol Wells • April Young • Larry Zerner

Center for the Study of Political Graphics
Farm Sanctuary • Gunk Foundation
National Lawyers Guild
Puffin Foundation • Resist
School of The Museum of Fine Arts, Boston
Social and Public Art Resource Center
Tanne Foundation
The Theater Offensive
Volunteer Lawyers for the Arts, CA
Volunteer Lawyers for the Arts, MA

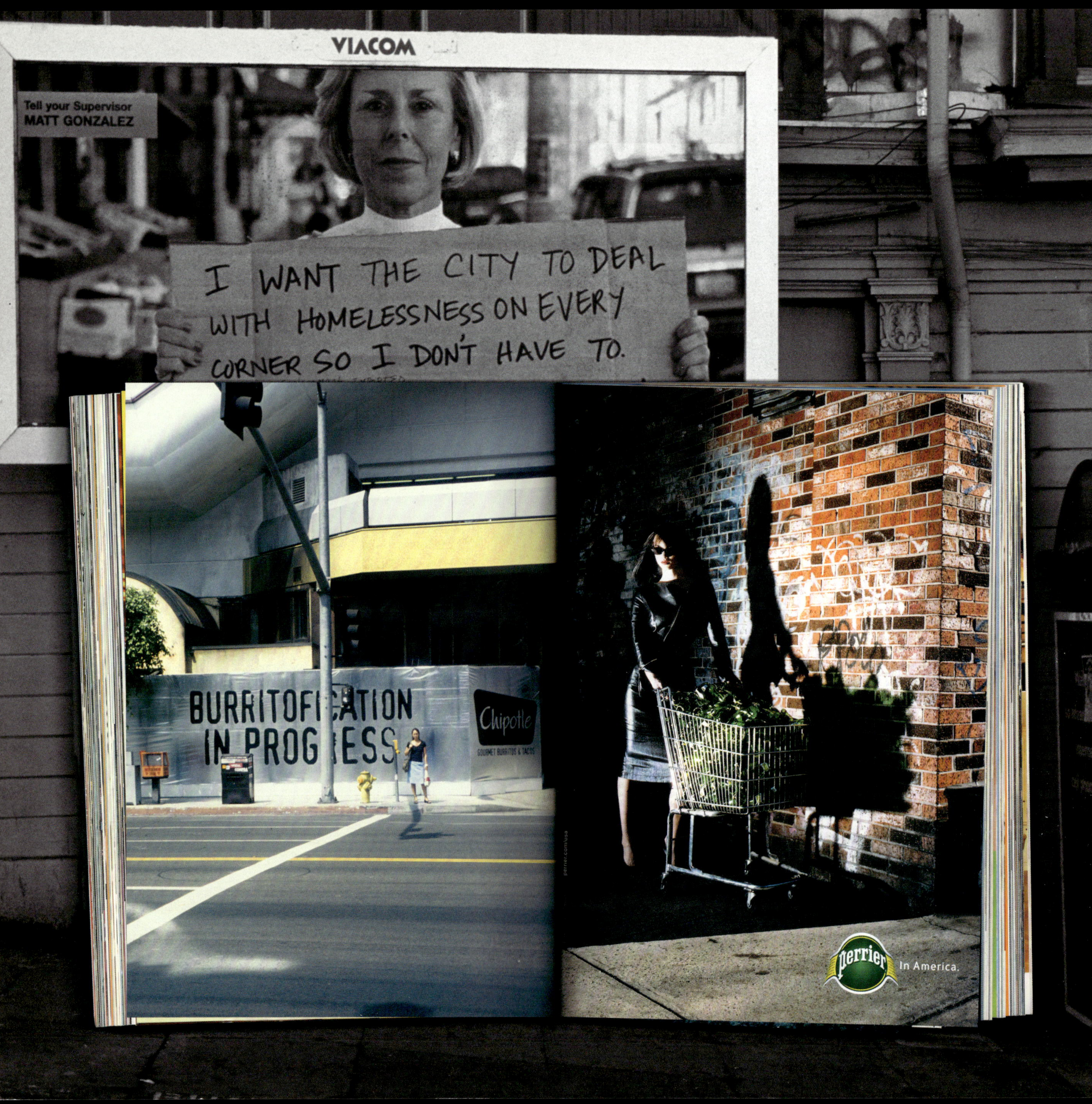
VIACOM
Tell your Supervisor
MATT GONZALEZ
I WANT THE CITY TO DEAL WITH HOMELESSNESS ON EVERY CORNER SO I DON'T HAVE TO.
BURRITOFICATION IN PROGRESS
Chipotle
GOURMET BURRITOS & TACOS
perrier
In America.

Left: *Sample #1 (Chipotle/Perrier/The Haight, San Francisco),* collage, dimensions variable, 2003. Right: *White Blight,* offset poster, 17x11 in, 1999.

Following pages
Left: *Economic Boom For Whom?,* documentation of billboard in Mattapan, MA, 1999. Right: *White Blight,* documentation of posters wheat-pasted on luxury loft construction, San Francisco, 1999.

WHITE BLIGHT

BULLDOZE THE PROJECTS, BUY A LOFT, DRINK A STARBUCKS, REVOKE WELFARE, EVICT A WORKING FAMILY, SHOP THE GAP, STEP OVER THE HOMELESS, DISPLACE QUEERS, GET A RETRIEVER, HIRE A MEXICAN MAID, PERSECUTE IMMIGRANTS, TUNE THE VOLVO, DEMOLISH AFFIRMATIVE ACTION, TAKE-OUT NOUVEAU CHINESE, HIRE MORE POLICE, GLORIFY GENTRIFICATION & CALL IT COMMUNITY REVITALIZATION.

ECONOMIC BOOM FOR WHOM?

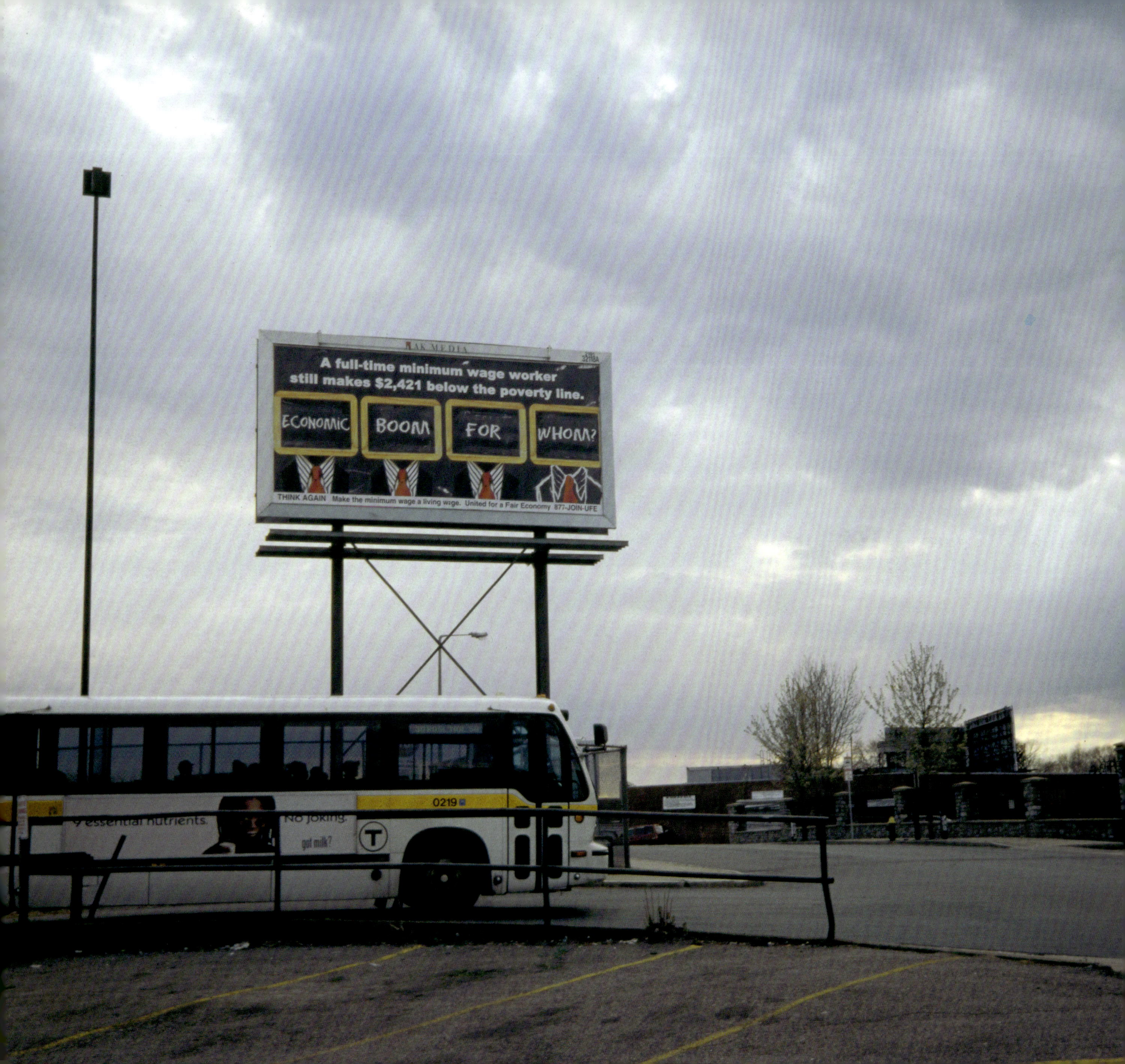
AK MEDIA
A full-time minimum wage worker still makes $2,421 below the poverty line.
ECONOMIC
BOOM
FOR
WHOM?
THINK AGAIN   Make the minimum wage a living wage.   United for a Fair Economy   877-JOIN-UFE
9 essential nutrients.
No joking.
got milk?
T
0219

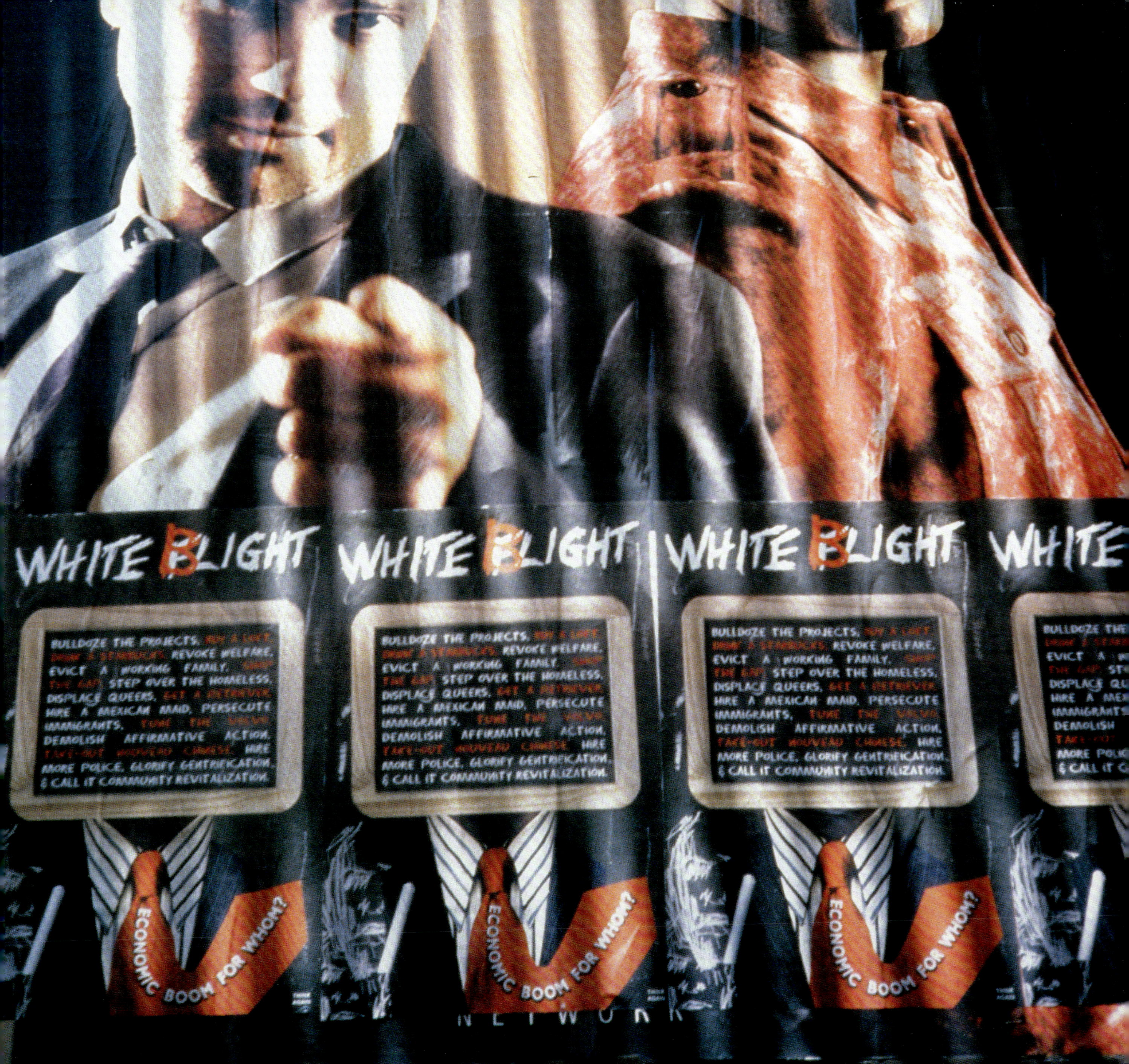

WHITE BLIGHT
BULLDOZE THE PROJECTS, BUY A LOFT, DRINK A STARBUCKS, REVOKE WELFARE, EVICT A WORKING FAMILY, SHOP THE GAP, STEP OVER THE HOMELESS, DISPLACE QUEERS, GET A RETRIEVER, HIRE A MEXICAN MAID, PERSECUTE IMMIGRANTS, TUNE THE VOLVO, DEMOLISH AFFIRMATIVE ACTION, TAKE-OUT NOUVEAU CHINESE, HIRE MORE POLICE, GLORIFY GENTRIFICATION, & CALL IT COMMUNITY REVITALIZATION.
ECONOMIC BOOM FOR WHOM?
NETWORK

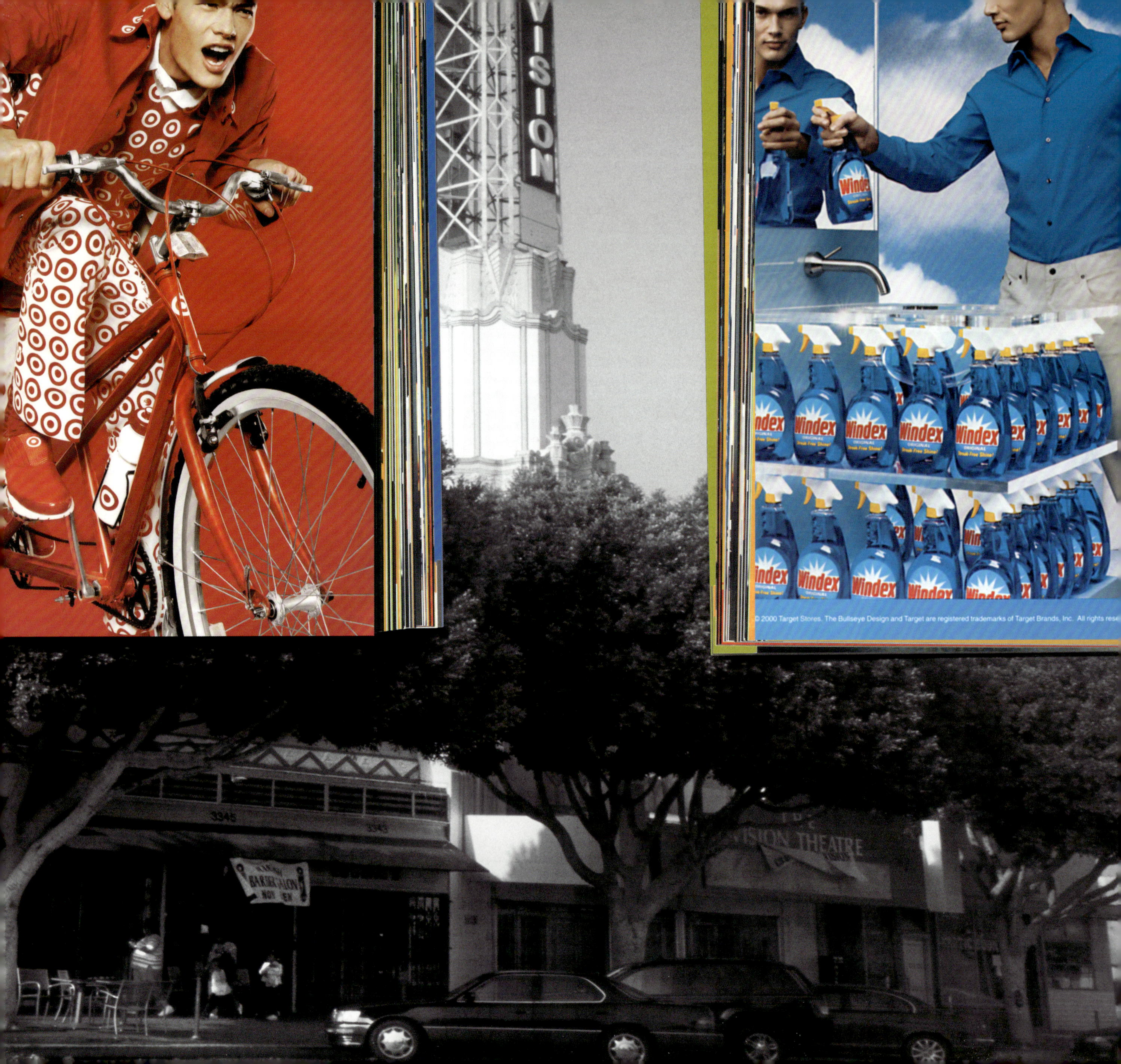
Windex
ORIGINAL
Streak Free Shine!
VISION
3345
VISION THEATRE

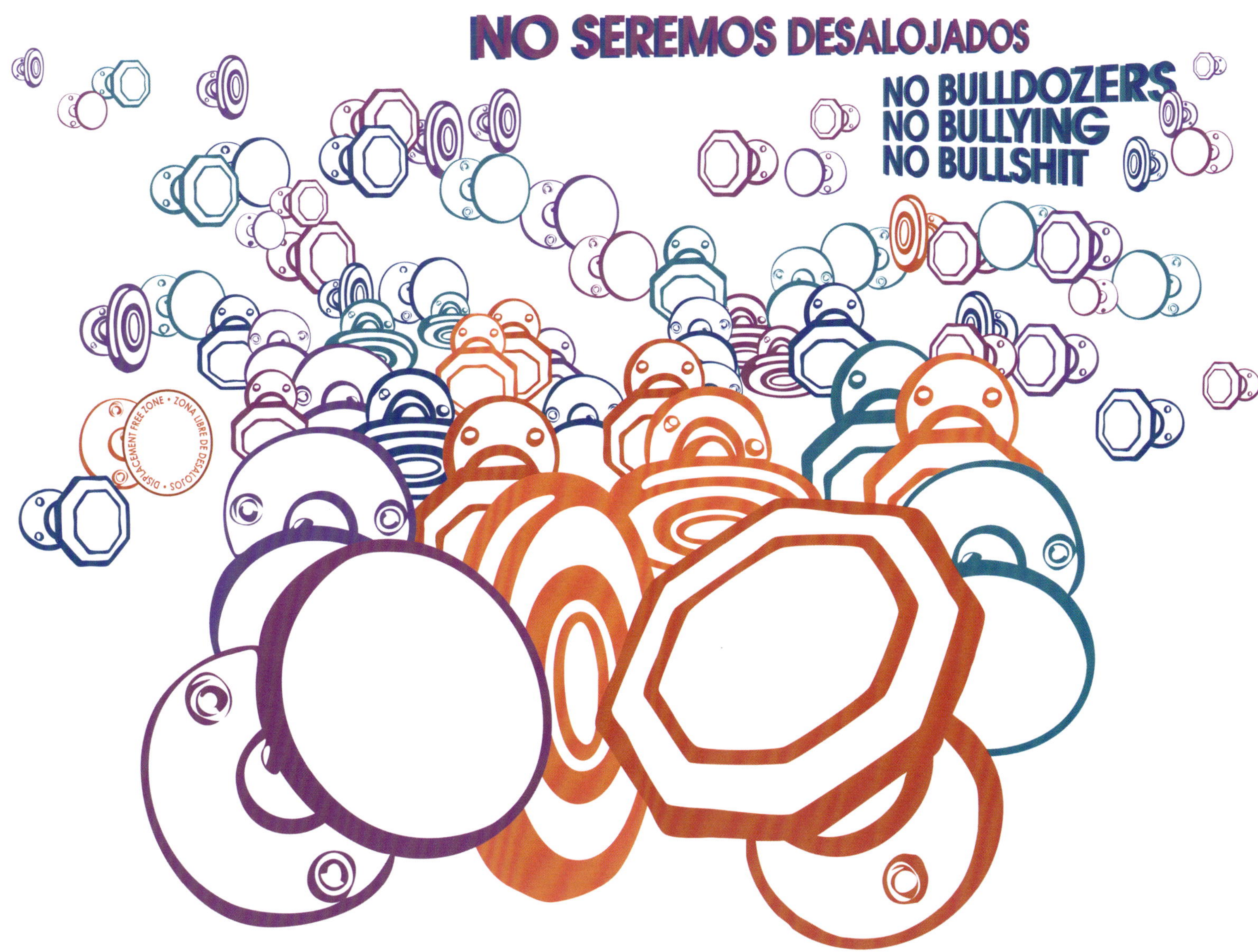

NO SEREMOS DESALOJADOS
NO BULLDOZERS
NO BULLYING
NO BULLSHIT
DISPLACEMENT FREE ZONE · ZONA LIBRE DE DESALOJOS ·

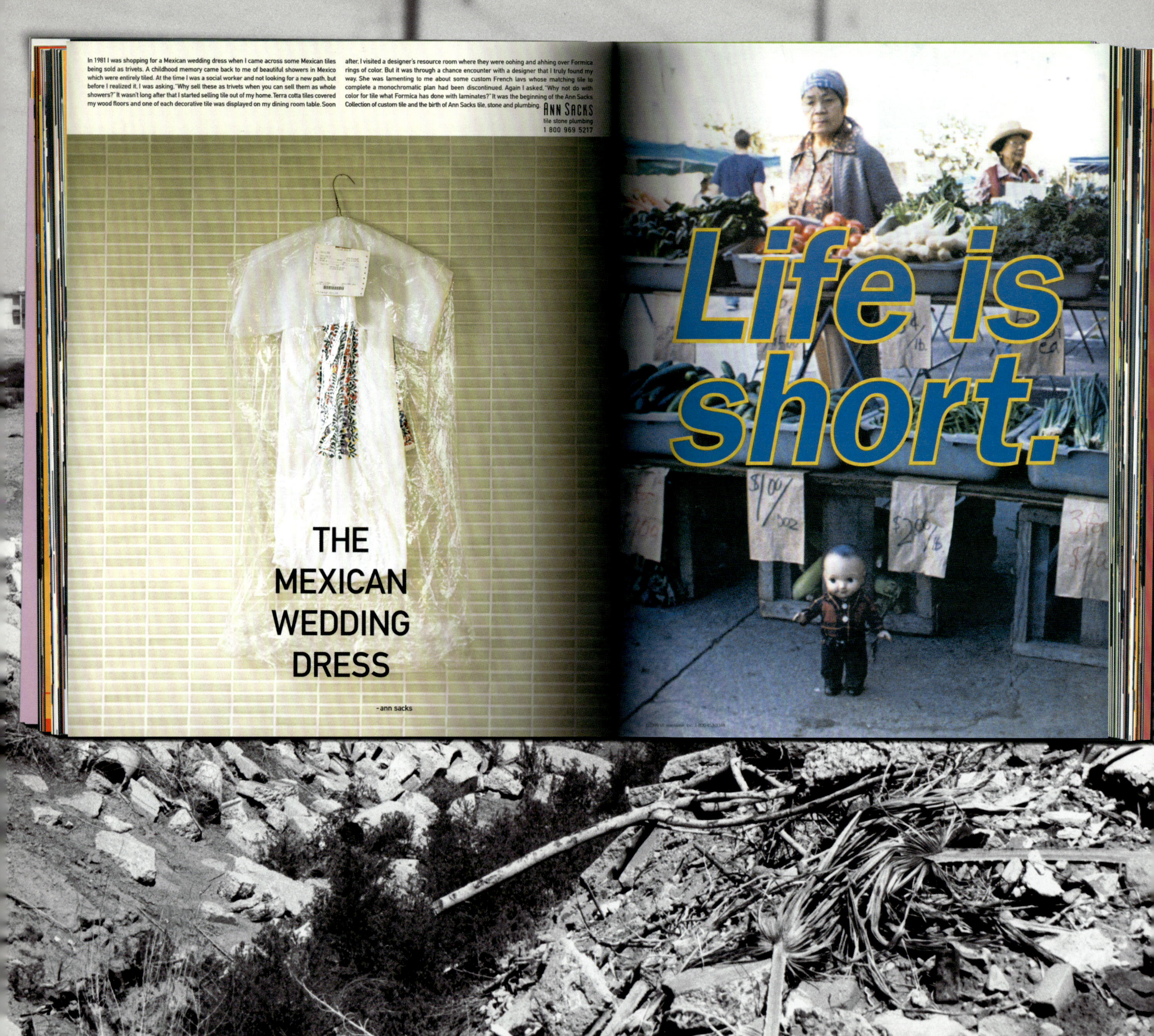

In 1981 I was shopping for a Mexican wedding dress when I came across some Mexican tiles being sold as trivets. A childhood memory came back to me of beautiful showers in Mexico which were entirely tiled. At the time I was a social worker and not looking for a new path, but before I realized it, I was asking, "Why sell these as trivets when you can sell them as whole showers?" It wasn't long after that I started selling tile out of my home. Terra cotta tiles covered my wood floors and one of each decorative tile was displayed on my dining room table. Soon after, I visited a designer's resource room where they were oohing and ahhing over Formica rings of color. But it was through a chance encounter with a designer that I truly found my way. She was lamenting to me about some custom French lavs whose matching tile to complete a monochromatic plan had been discontinued. Again I asked, "Why not do with color for tile what Formica has done with laminates?" It was the beginning of the Ann Sacks Collection of custom tile and the birth of Ann Sacks tile, stone and plumbing.

ANN SACKS
tile stone plumbing
1 800 969 5217

THE
MEXICAN
WEDDING
DRESS

- ann sacks

Life is
short.

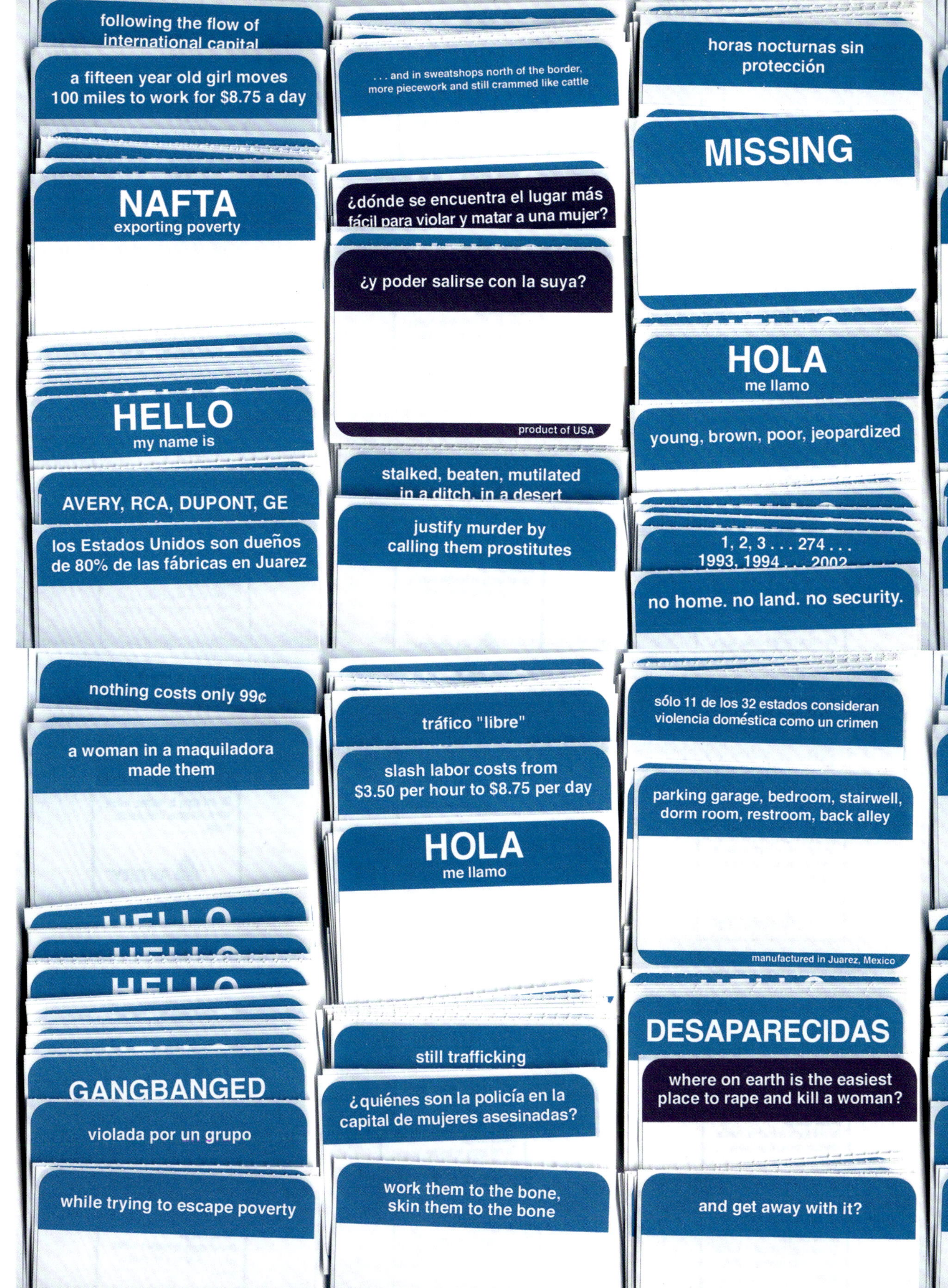

Preceding pages
Left: *Sample #2 (Target/Target/ Leimert Park, Los Angeles)*, collage, dimensions variable, 2003. Right: *No Bullshit,* silkscreen poster, 20x26 in, 2002.

Left: *Sample #3 (Ann Sacks/VF Jeanswear/Cuidad Juarez, Mexico)*, collage, dimensions variable, 2003. Right: *Hello/Hola,* postcard, 6x8 in; wall installation, 10x15 ft, 2002.

Cuidad Juarez photo: Jennifer Araujo

A woman in a sweatshop made them.

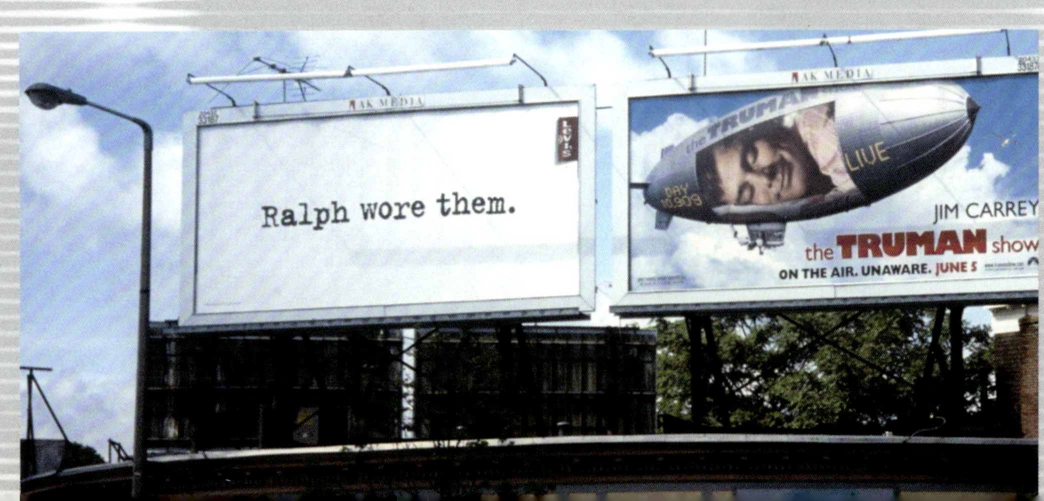

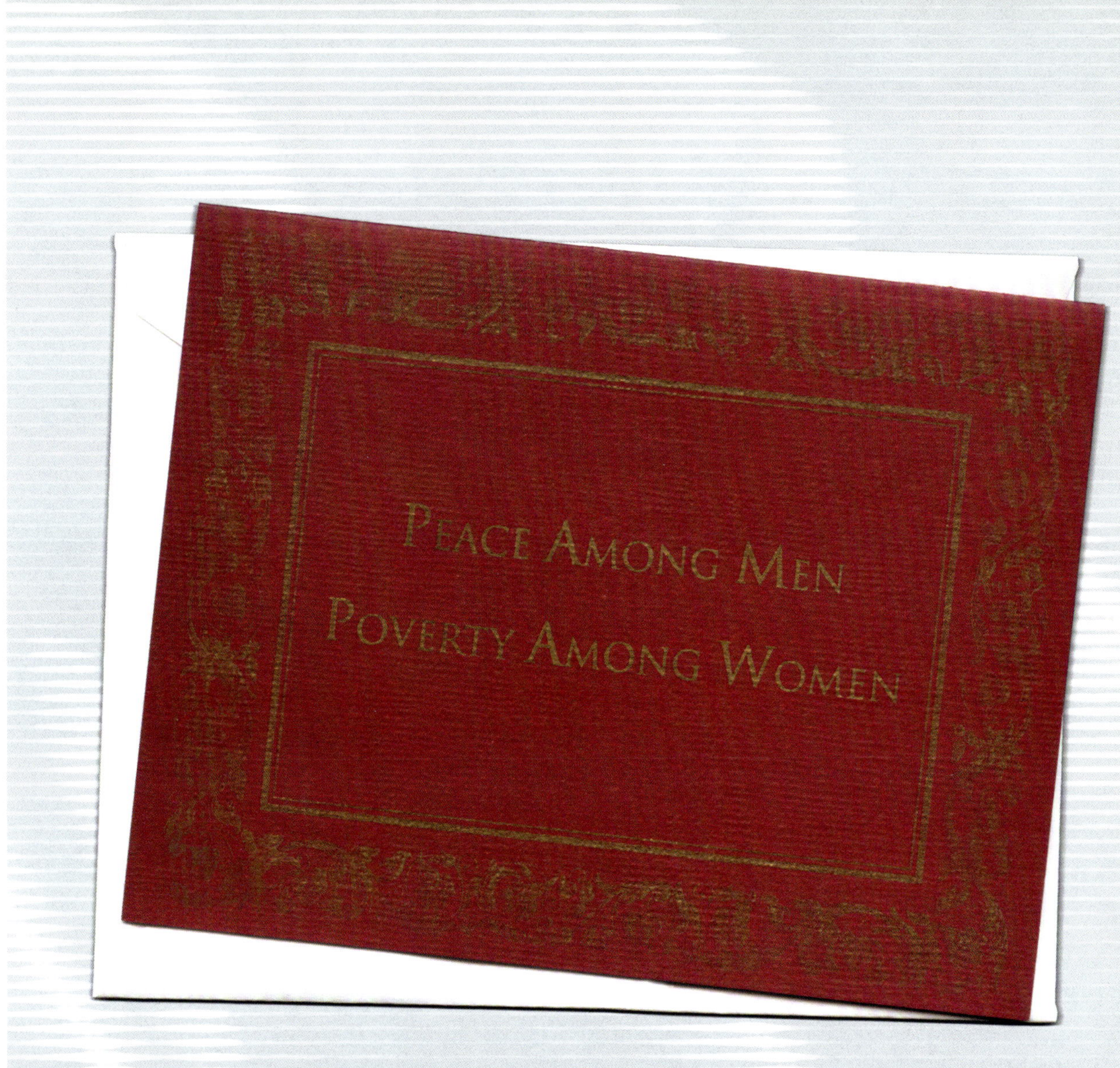

Left: *A Woman In A Sweatshop,* postcard, 4x6 in, 1998. Left below: Documentation of Levi's ad campaign, Boston, 1998. Right: *Poverty Among Women,* holiday card, 4x6 in, 1998. Right below: Detail of holiday card interior.

Following pages
Left: *Sample #4 (Lunch Line/American Dog/Hog Farm, Location Unknown),* collage, dimensions variable, 2003. Right: *Human Abuse Of Animals,* holiday card, 6x4 in, 1999.

Lunch photo: Jacquelyn C. Black; Hog Farm photo: Farm Sanctuary

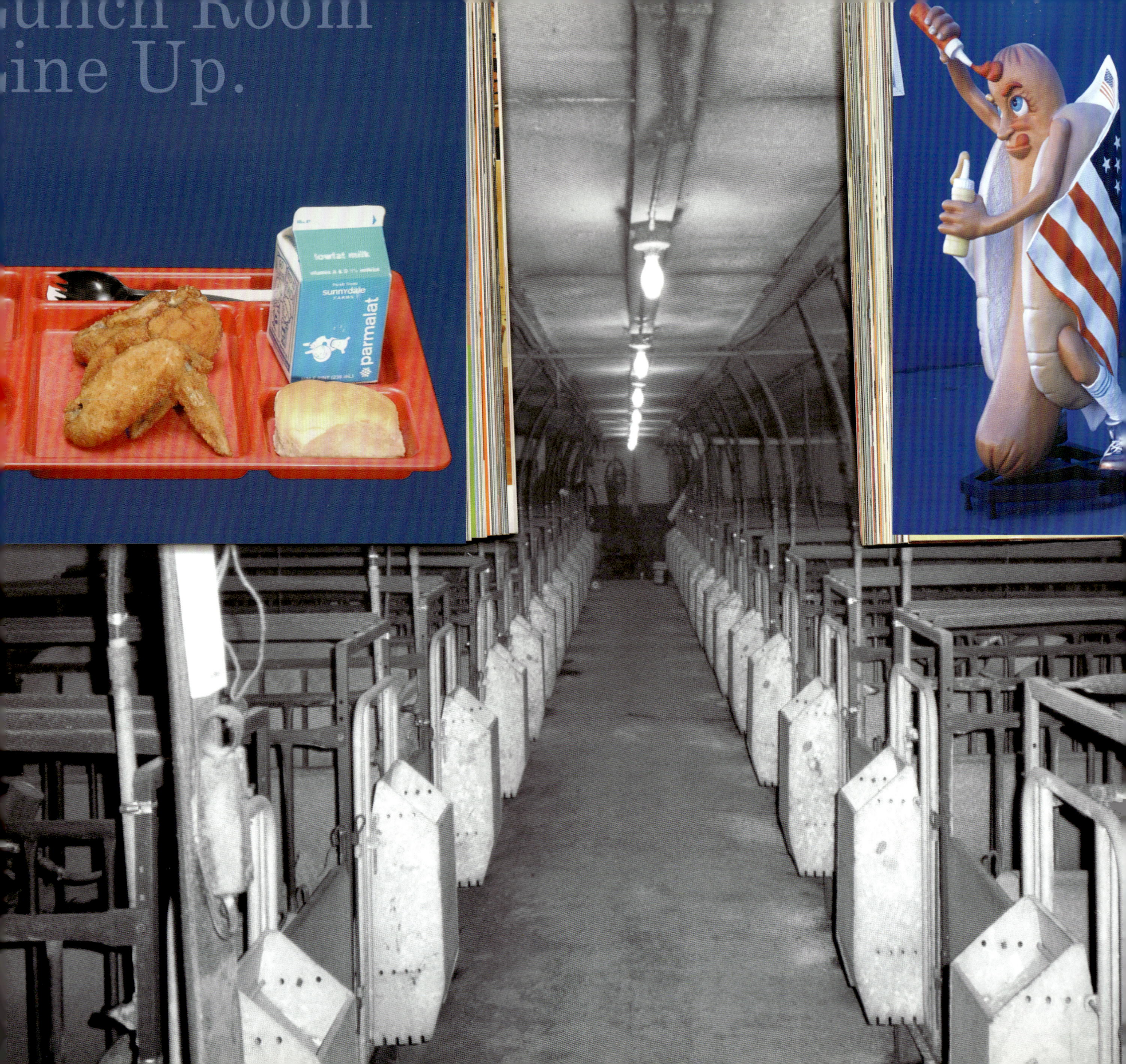

Lunch Room
Line Up.
lowfat milk
vitamins A & D 1% milkfat
fresh from
sunnydale
FARMS
parmalat

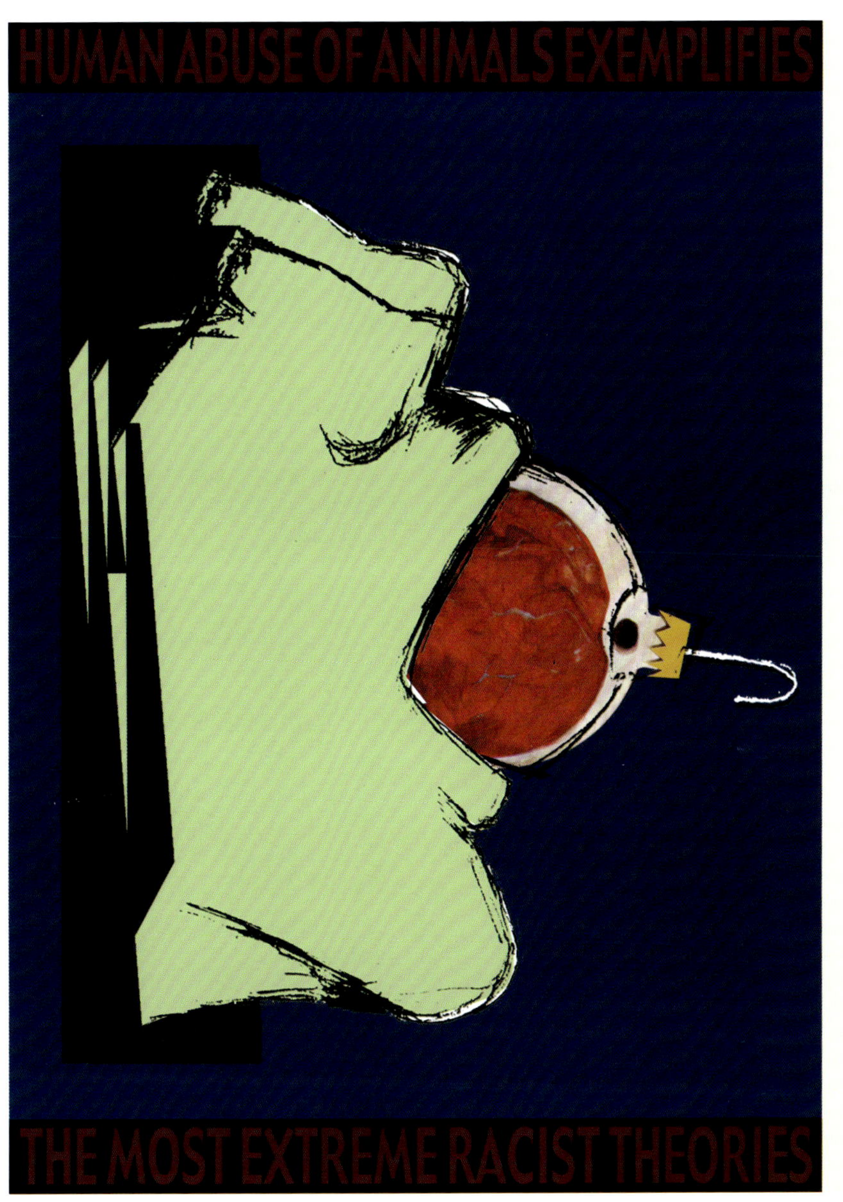

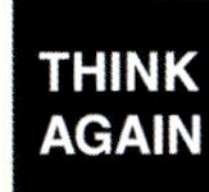

CHECKLIST FOR GATHERING AT THE HOLIDAY TABLE

- ☐ stop uncle when he cracks a racist joke
- ☐ speak up when nephew asks: "how do lesbians have sex?"
- ☐ question mom when she complains that "those Koreans" are ruining the neighborhood
- ☐ go ballistic when dad credits the drug companies for stopping AIDS
- ☐ cough loudly when sister's fiance refers to the death penalty as "justice"
- ☐ remind everyone that 8 billion animals are killed every year for human consumption, and that most are systematically confined, force-fed, amputated and electrocuted in factory farms

THINK AGAIN object to the abuse of animals and stop eating meat

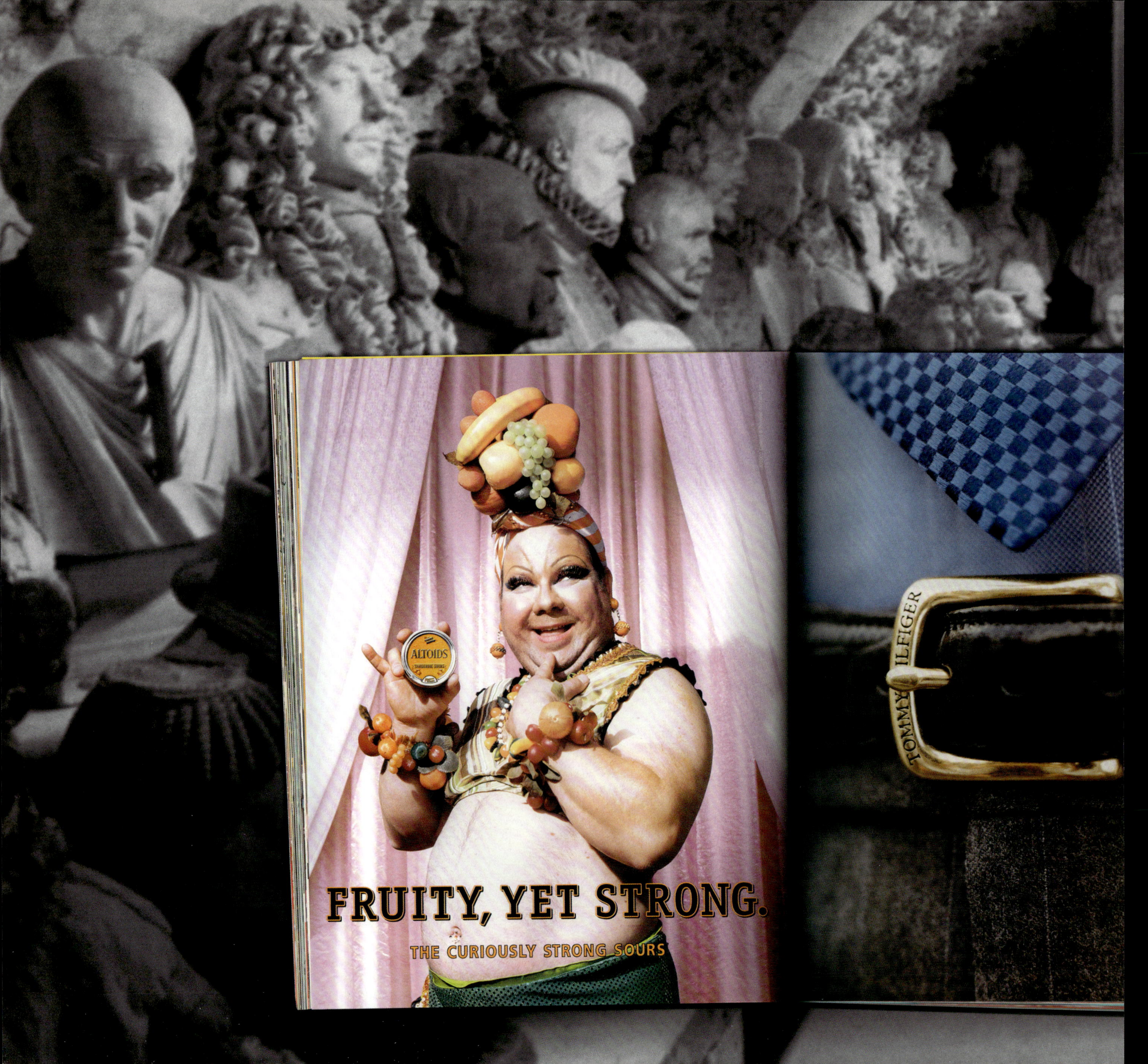

ALTOIDS
FRUITY, YET STRONG.
THE CURIOUSLY STRONG SOURS
TOMMY HILFIGER

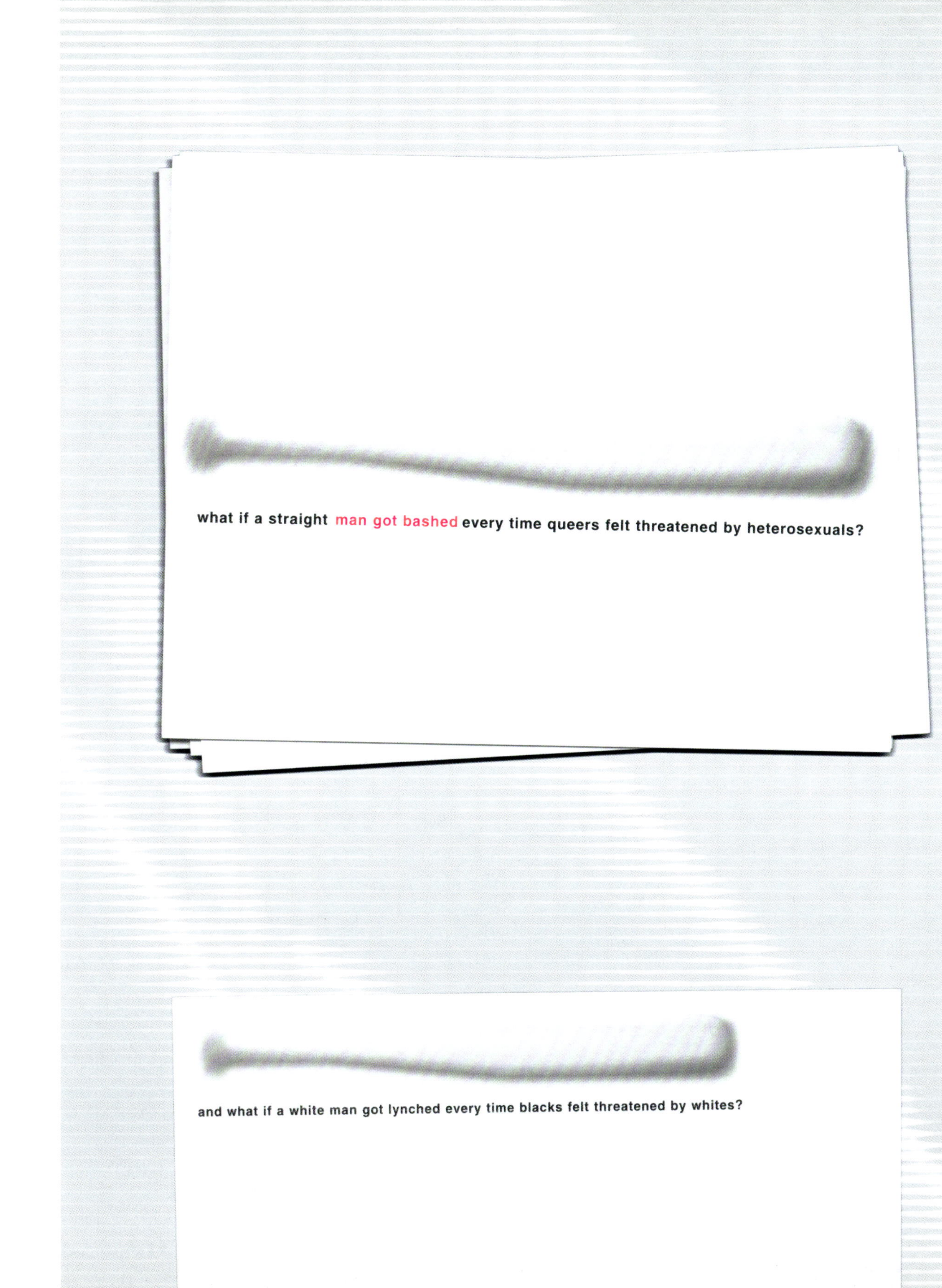

Left: *Sample #5 (Altoids/Tommy Hilfiger/ Museum Storage, Location Unknown),* collage, dimensions variable, 2003. Right: *Bash Bat,* postcard, 4x6 in, 1999.

Following pages
Left: *Popping The Question* (truck 1 of 2), documentation of mobile billboard caravan at San Francisco's City Hall, Valentine's Day, 2000. Right: *Popping The Question* (truck 2 of 2), documentation of mobile billboard caravan, San Francisco, 2000.

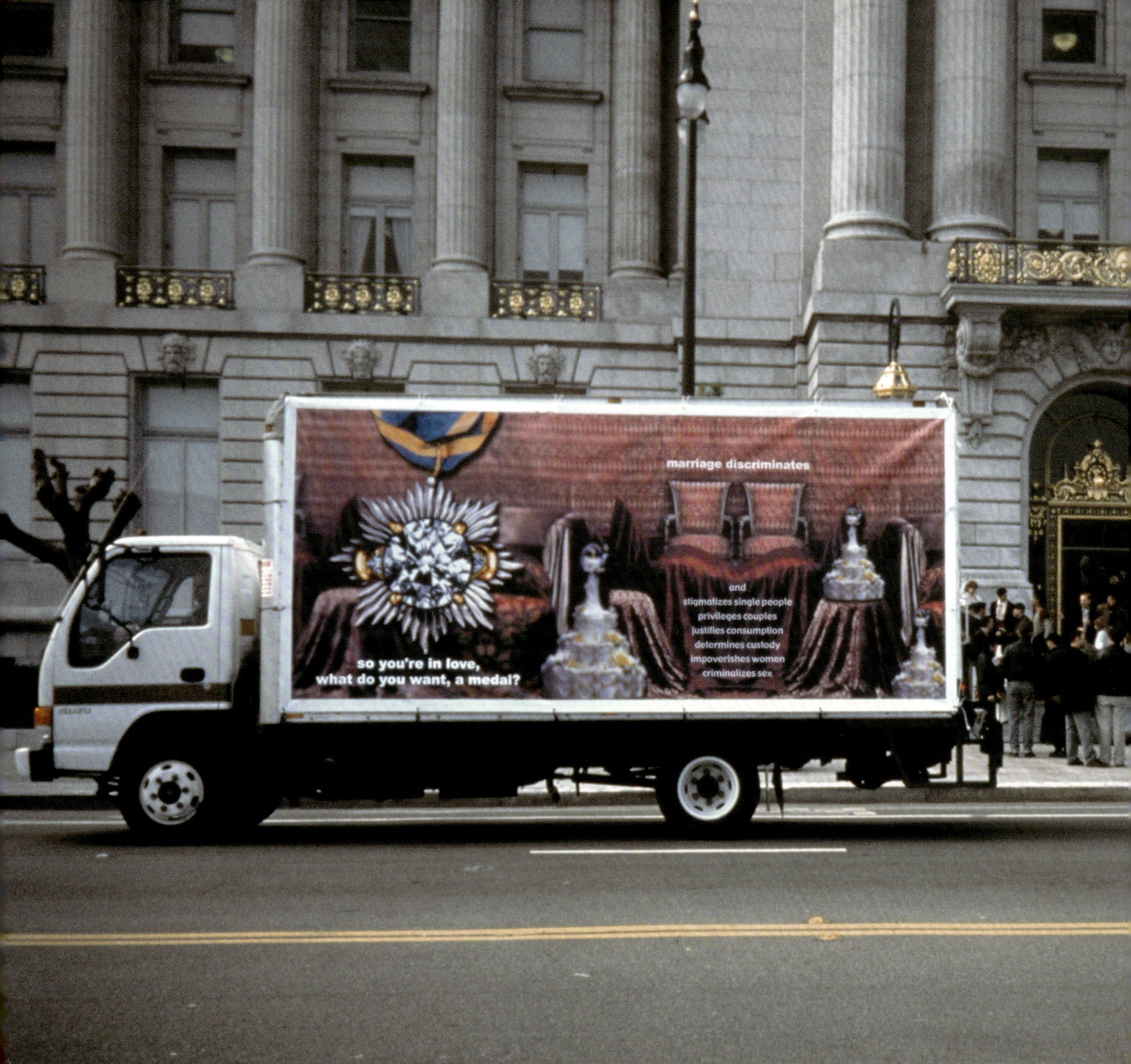
marriage discriminates
so you're in love,
what do you want, a medal?
and
stigmatizes single people
privileges couples
justifies consumption
determines custody
impoverishes women
criminalizes sex
ISUZU

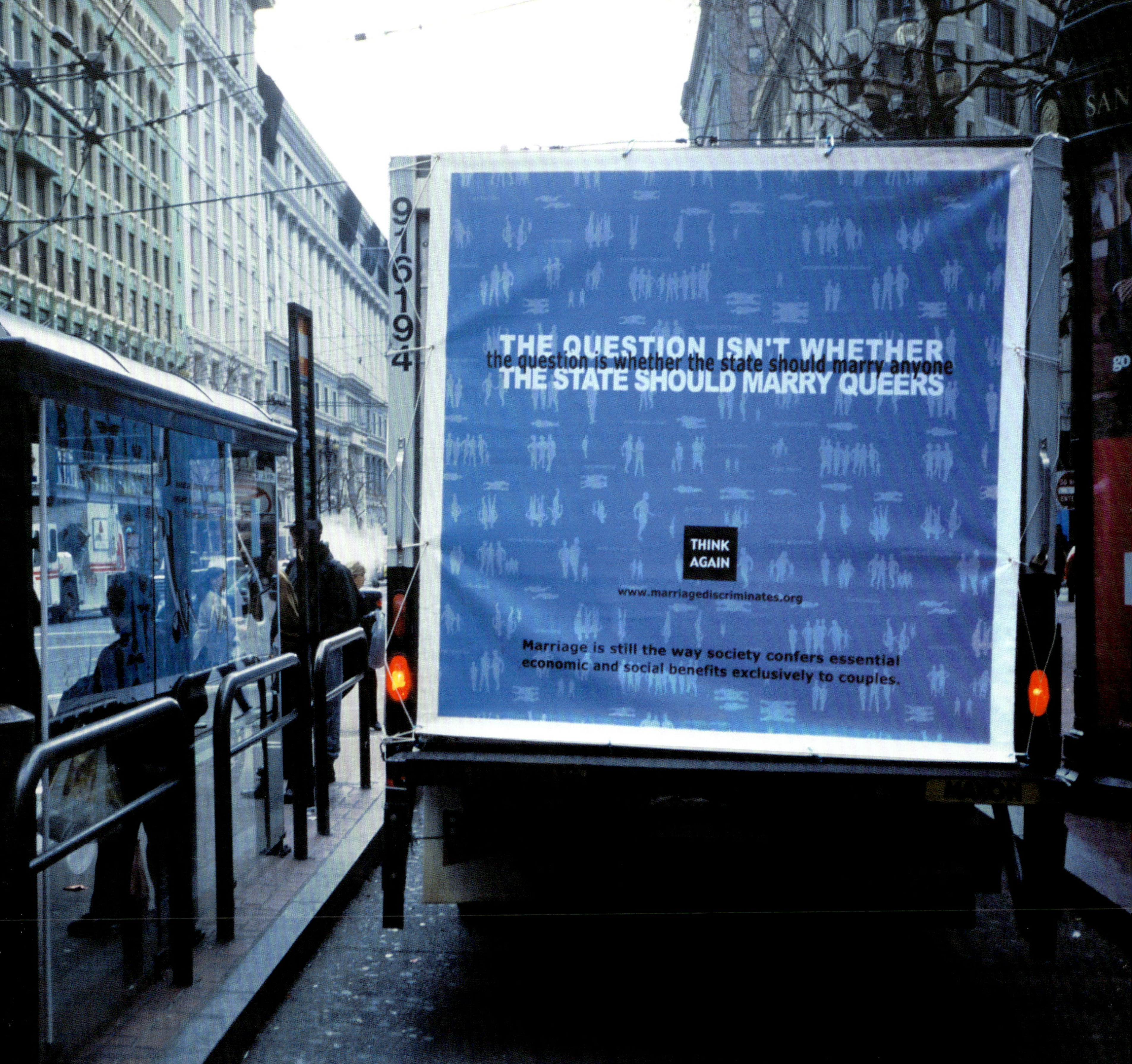
91619 4
THE QUESTION ISN'T WHETHER
the question is whether the state should marry anyone
THE STATE SHOULD MARRY QUEERS
THINK
AGAIN
www.marriagediscriminates.org
Marriage is still the way society confers essential
economic and social benefits exclusively to couples.

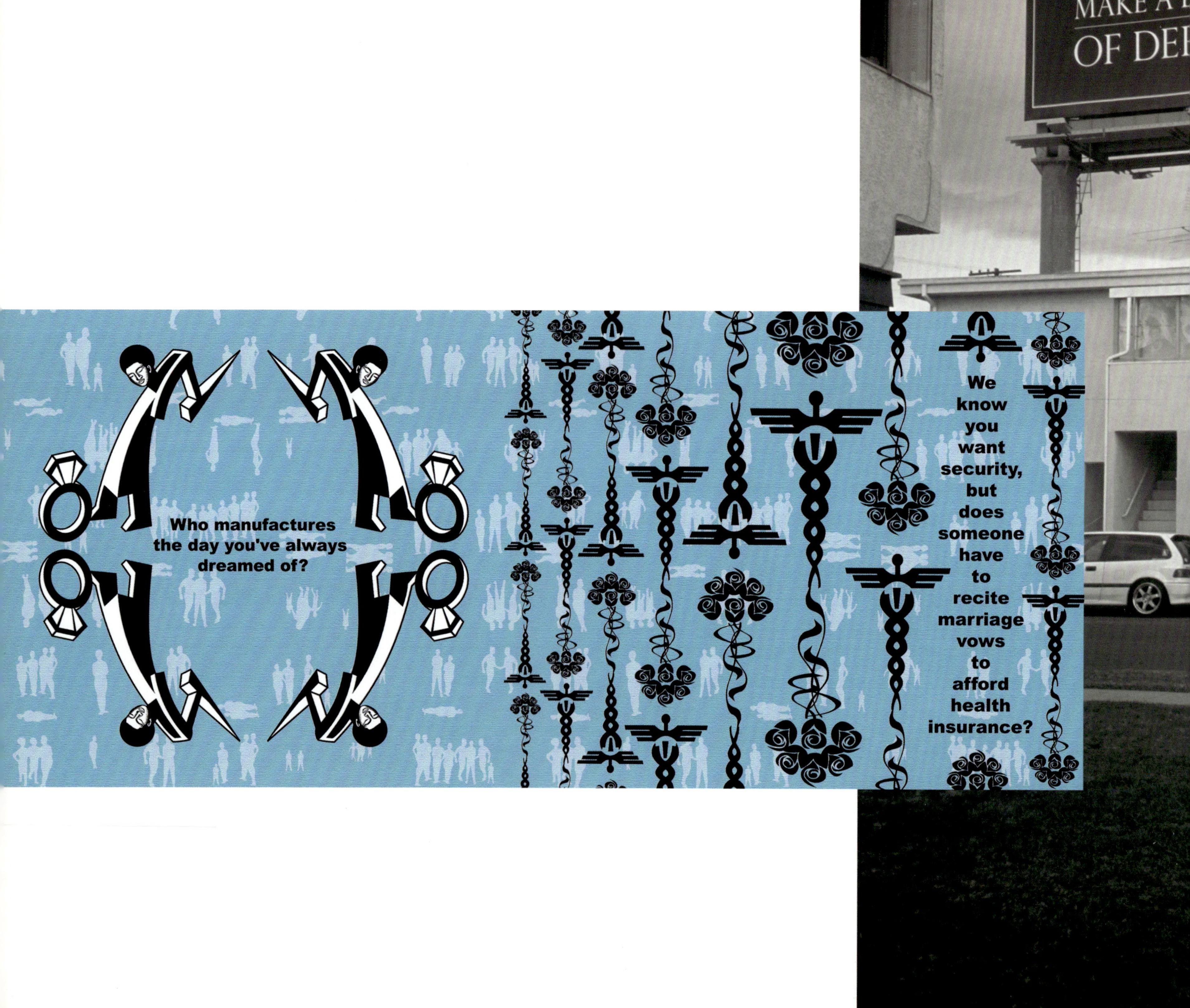

MAKE A D[...]
OF DE[...]
Who manufactures
the day you've always
dreamed of?
We
know
you
want
security,
but
does
someone
have
to
recite
marriage
vows
to
afford
health
insurance?

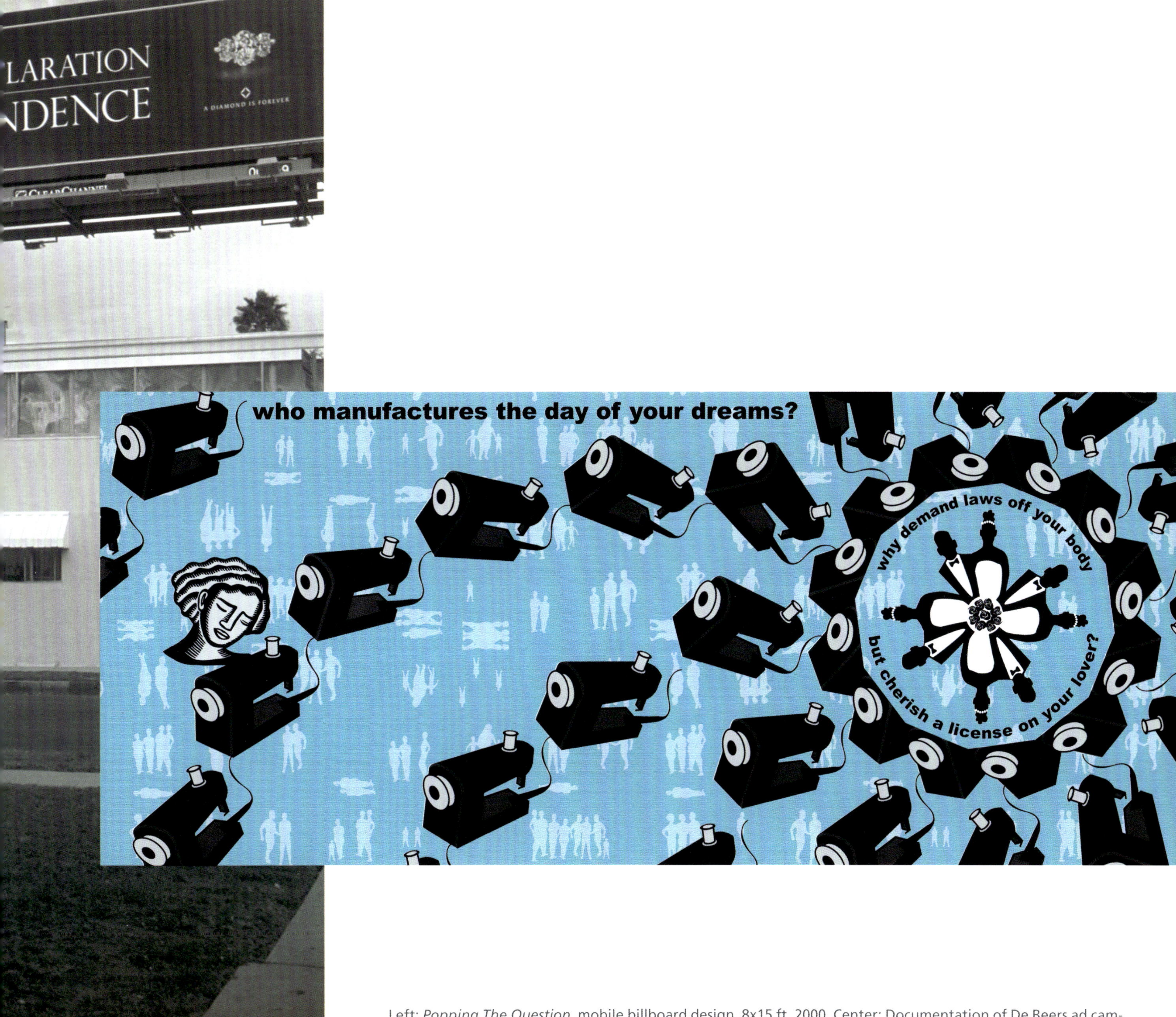

Left: *Popping The Question,* mobile billboard design, 8x15 ft, 2000. Center: Documentation of De Beers ad campaign, Los Angeles, 2003. Right: *Popping The Question,* mobile billboard design, 8x15 ft, 2000.

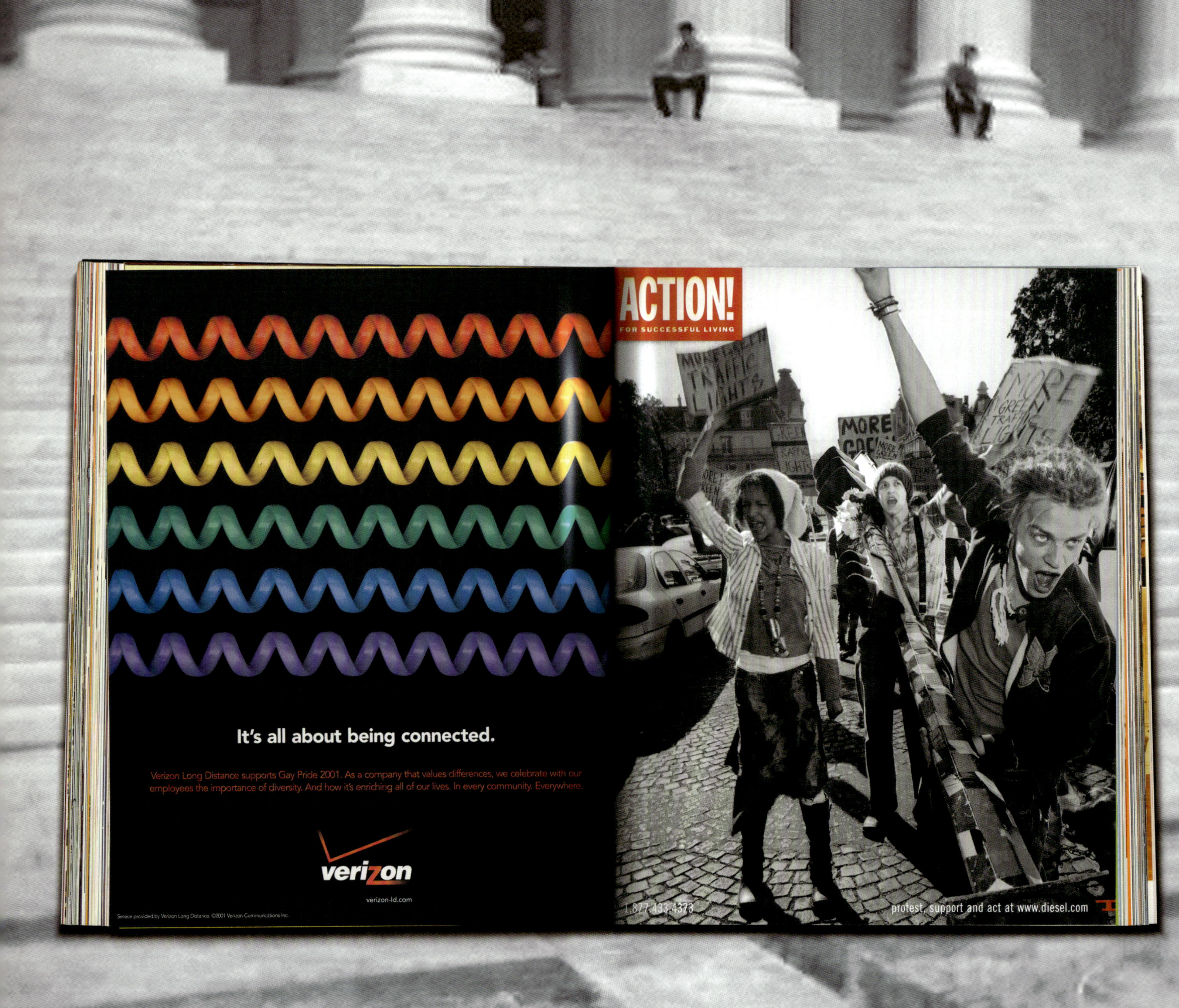
It's all about being connected.

Verizon Long Distance supports Gay Pride 2001. As a company that values differences, we celebrate with our employees the importance of diversity. And how it's enriching all of our lives. In every community. Everywhere.

verizon

verizon-ld.com

Service provided by Verizon Long Distance. ©2001 Verizon Communications Inc.

ACTION!
FOR SUCCESSFUL LIVING

MORE GREEN TRAFFIC LIGHTS
MORE GREEN TRAFFIC LIGHTS
GREEN TRAFFIC LIGHTS
MORE GREEN

1 877 433 4373

protest, support and act at www.diesel.com

Left: *Sample #6 (Verizon/Diesel/Sodomy Criminalized in 1986 and Legalized in 2003, Washington, DC),* collage, dimensions variable, 2003. Right: *Target Marketing Is Not A Social Movement* (front), postcard, 6x4 in, 2001.

Following pages
Left: *Advertising Works Because You Don't Think It Does* and *Target Marketing Is Not A Social Movement,* documentation of postcard rack intervention, Los Angeles, 2001. Right: Detail of *Target Marketing Is Not A Social Movement* (back) *and Advertising Works Because You Don't Think It Does* (back), 2001.

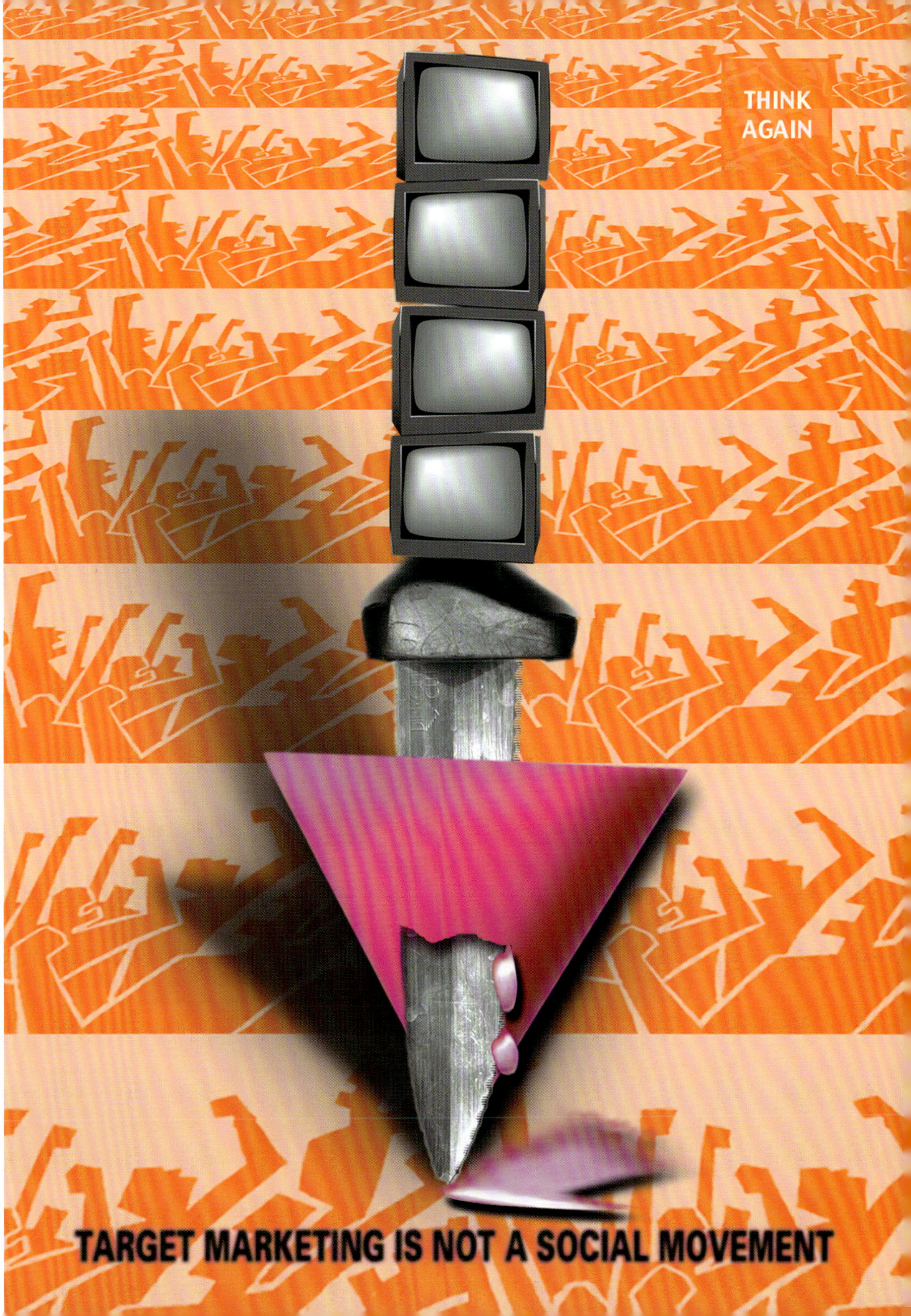

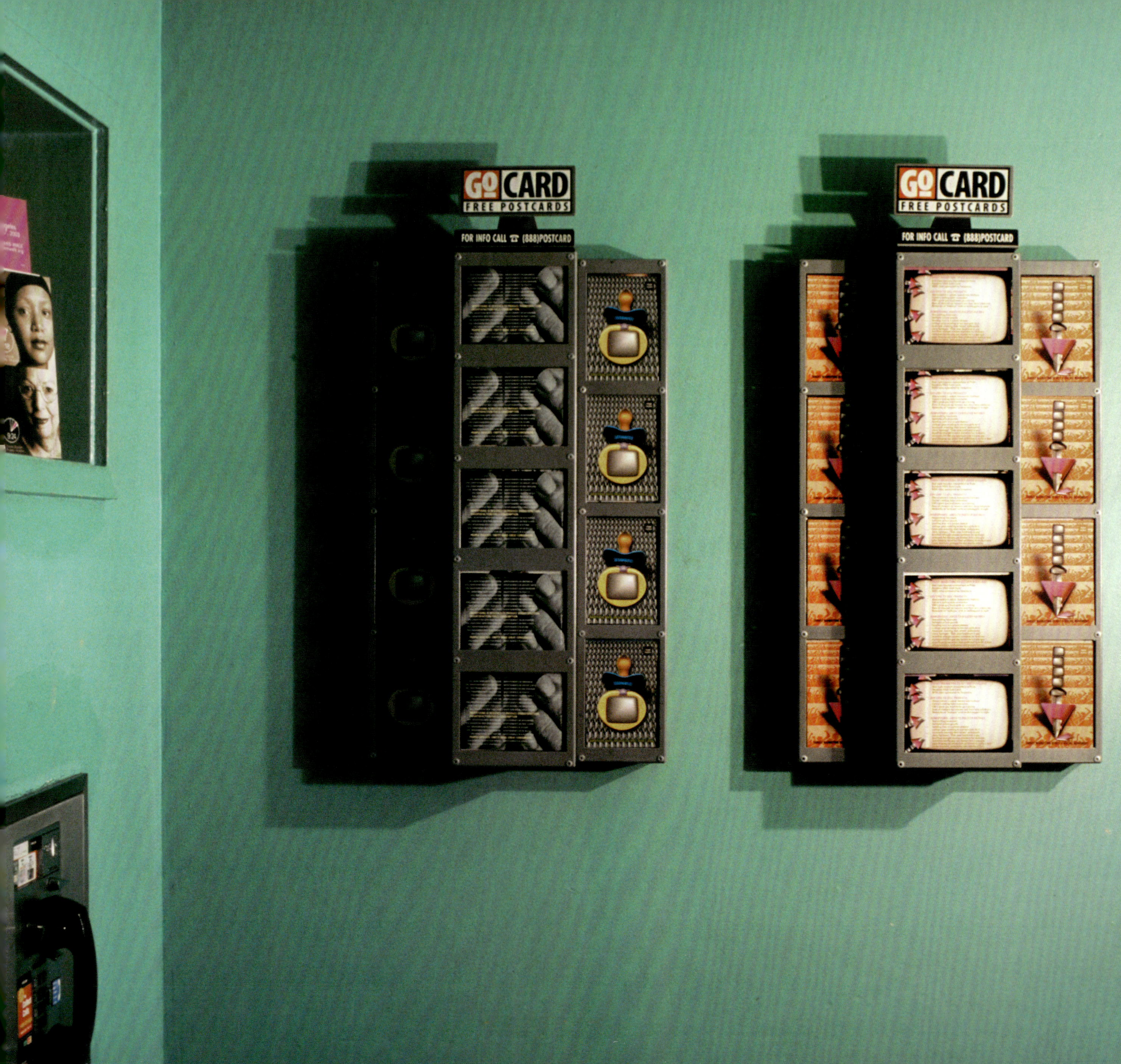
GO CARD
FREE POSTCARDS
FOR INFO CALL ☎ (888)POSTCARD
GO CARD
FREE POSTCARDS
FOR INFO CALL ☎ (888)POSTCARD

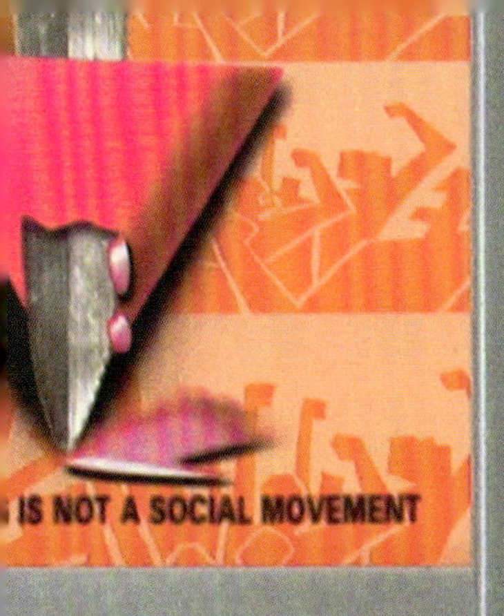
IS NOT A SOCIAL MOVEMENT

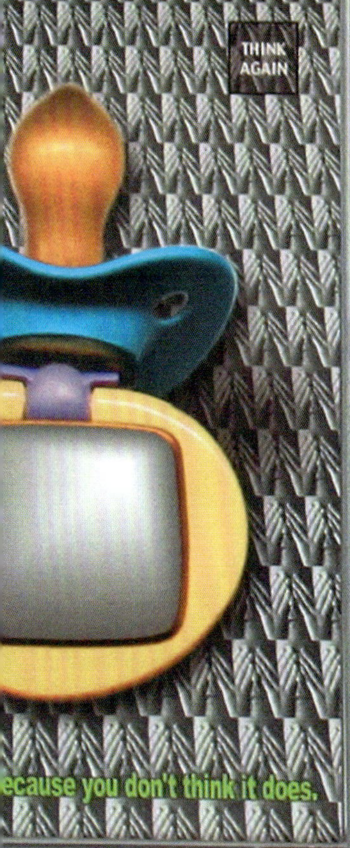
THINK
AGAIN

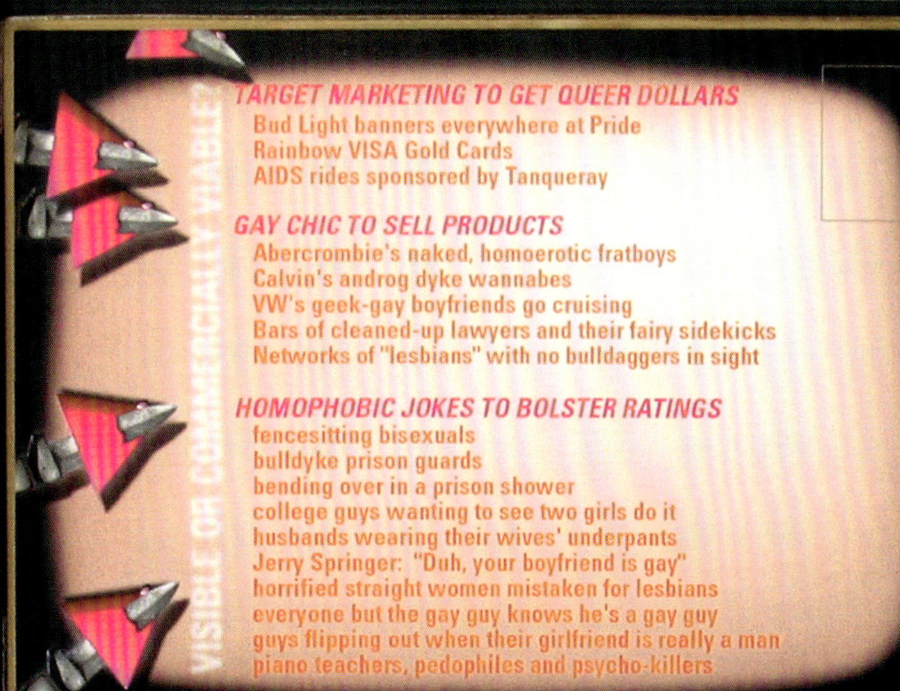
VISIBLE OR COMMERCIALLY VIABLE?

TARGET MARKETING TO GET QUEER DOLLARS
Bud Light banners everywhere at Pride
Rainbow VISA Gold Cards
AIDS rides sponsored by Tanqueray

GAY CHIC TO SELL PRODUCTS
Abercrombie's naked, homoerotic fratboys
Calvin's androg dyke wannabes
VW's geek-gay boyfriends go cruising
Bars of cleaned-up lawyers and their fairy sidekicks
Networks of "lesbians" with no bulldaggers in sight

HOMOPHOBIC JOKES TO BOLSTER RATINGS
fencesitting bisexuals
bulldyke prison guards
bending over in a prison shower
college guys wanting to see two girls do it
husbands wearing their wives' underpants
Jerry Springer: "Duh, your boyfriend is gay"
horrified straight women mistaken for lesbians
everyone but the gay guy knows he's a gay guy
guys flipping out when their girlfriend is really a man
piano teachers, pedophiles and psycho-killers

THINK AGAIN 2001 www.AgitArt.org

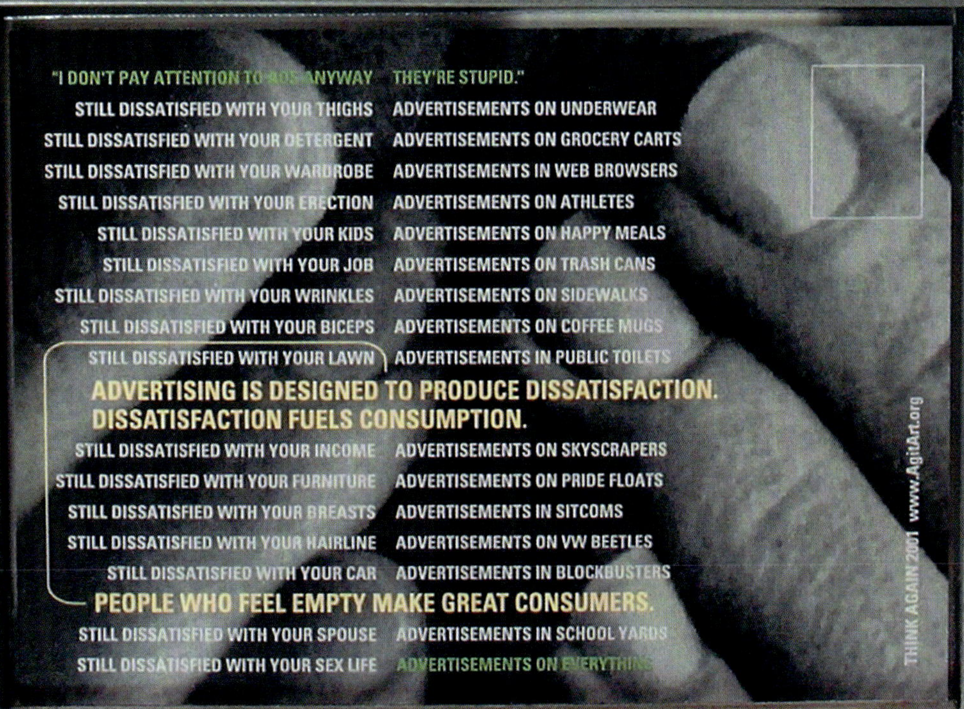
"I DON'T PAY ATTENTION TO ADS ANYWAY   THEY'RE STUPID."
STILL DISSATISFIED WITH YOUR THIGHS   ADVERTISEMENTS ON UNDERWEAR
STILL DISSATISFIED WITH YOUR DETERGENT   ADVERTISEMENTS ON GROCERY CARTS
STILL DISSATISFIED WITH YOUR WARDROBE   ADVERTISEMENTS IN WEB BROWSERS
STILL DISSATISFIED WITH YOUR ERECTION   ADVERTISEMENTS ON ATHLETES
STILL DISSATISFIED WITH YOUR KIDS   ADVERTISEMENTS ON HAPPY MEALS
STILL DISSATISFIED WITH YOUR JOB   ADVERTISEMENTS ON TRASH CANS
STILL DISSATISFIED WITH YOUR WRINKLES   ADVERTISEMENTS ON SIDEWALKS
STILL DISSATISFIED WITH YOUR BICEPS   ADVERTISEMENTS ON COFFEE MUGS
STILL DISSATISFIED WITH YOUR LAWN   ADVERTISEMENTS IN PUBLIC TOILETS

ADVERTISING IS DESIGNED TO PRODUCE DISSATISFACTION.
DISSATISFACTION FUELS CONSUMPTION.

STILL DISSATISFIED WITH YOUR INCOME   ADVERTISEMENTS ON SKYSCRAPERS
STILL DISSATISFIED WITH YOUR FURNITURE   ADVERTISEMENTS ON PRIDE FLOATS
STILL DISSATISFIED WITH YOUR BREASTS   ADVERTISEMENTS IN SITCOMS
STILL DISSATISFIED WITH YOUR HAIRLINE   ADVERTISEMENTS ON VW BEETLES
STILL DISSATISFIED WITH YOUR CAR   ADVERTISEMENTS IN BLOCKBUSTERS

PEOPLE WHO FEEL EMPTY MAKE GREAT CONSUMERS.

STILL DISSATISFIED WITH YOUR SPOUSE   ADVERTISEMENTS IN SCHOOL YARDS
STILL DISSATISFIED WITH YOUR SEX LIFE   ADVERTISEMENTS ON EVERYTHING

THINK AGAIN 2001 www.AgitArt.org

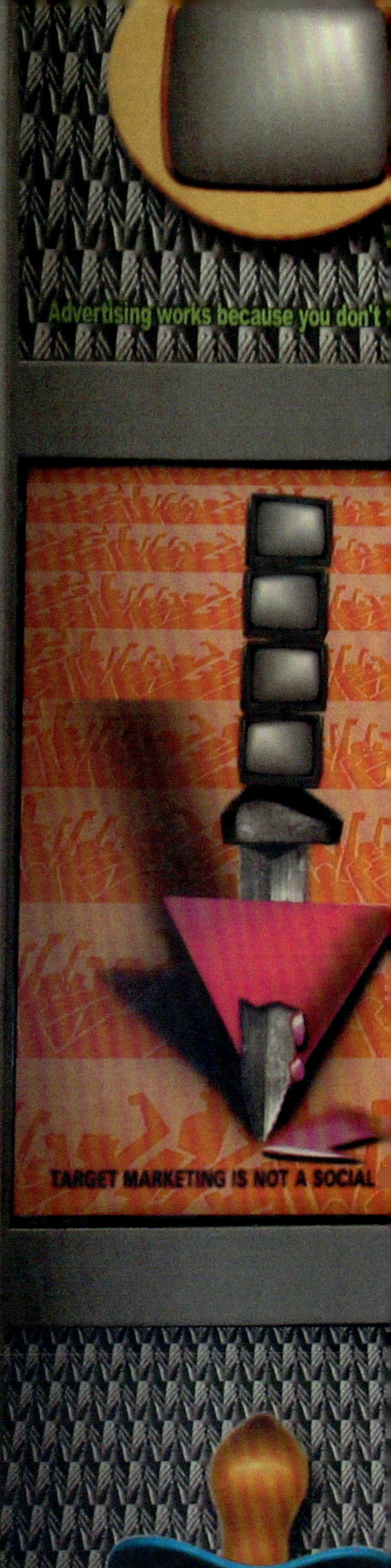
Advertising works because you don't
because you don't think it does.
THINK AGAIN
TARGET MARKETING IS NOT A SOCIAL

THINK AGAIN

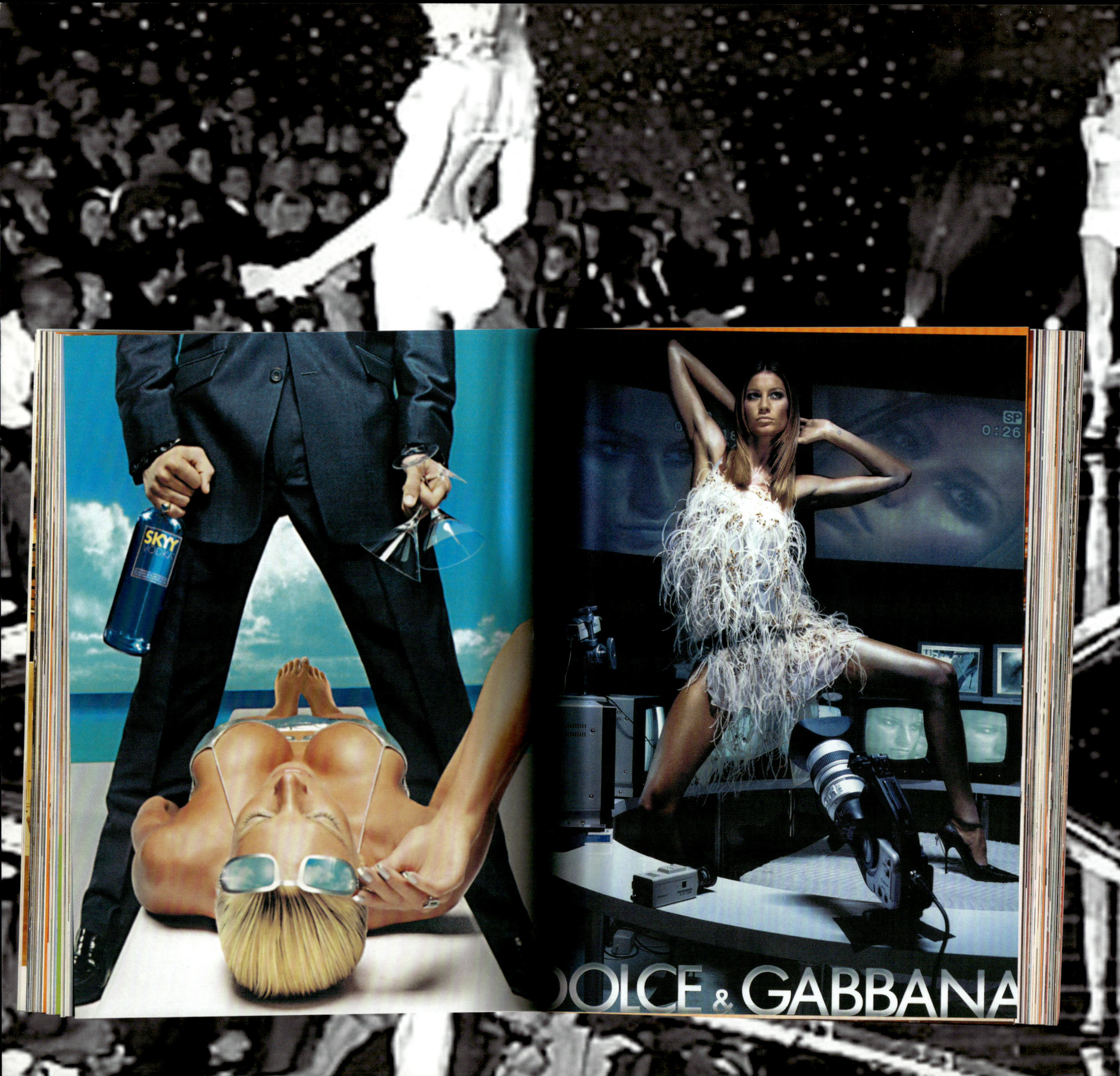

SKYY VODKA
SP 0:26
DOLCE & GABBANA

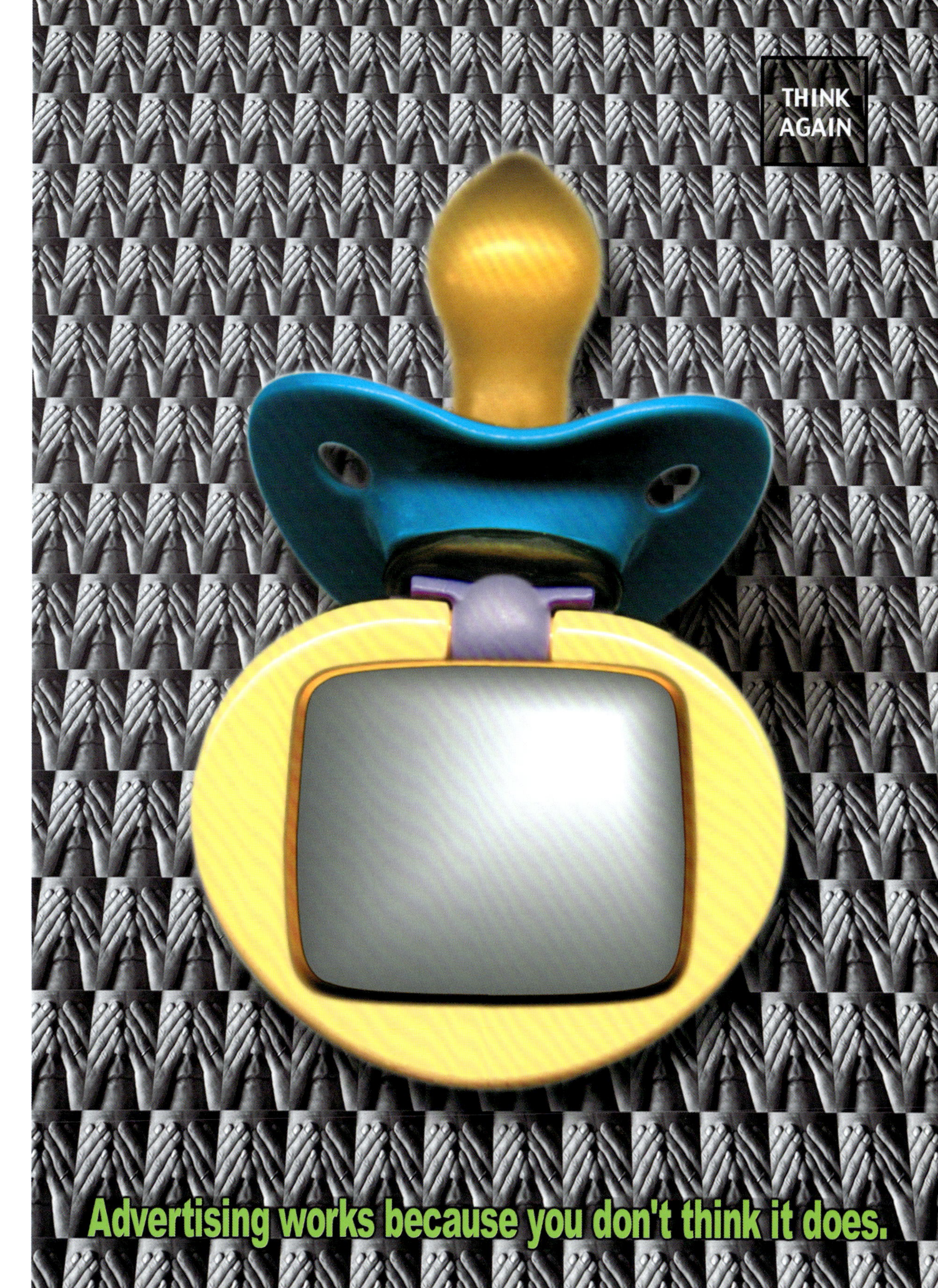

Left: *Sample #7 (Skyy/D&G/Victoria's Secret Fashion Show Telecast),* collage, dimensions variable, 2003. Right: *Advertising Works Because You Don't Think It Does* (front), postcard, 6x4 in, 2002.

Following pages
Left: *Sample #8 (Time/Time/CNN Broadcast Headquarters, New York City),* collage, dimensions variable, 2003. Right: *Televise An Alternative,* digital poster, dimensions variable, 2001.

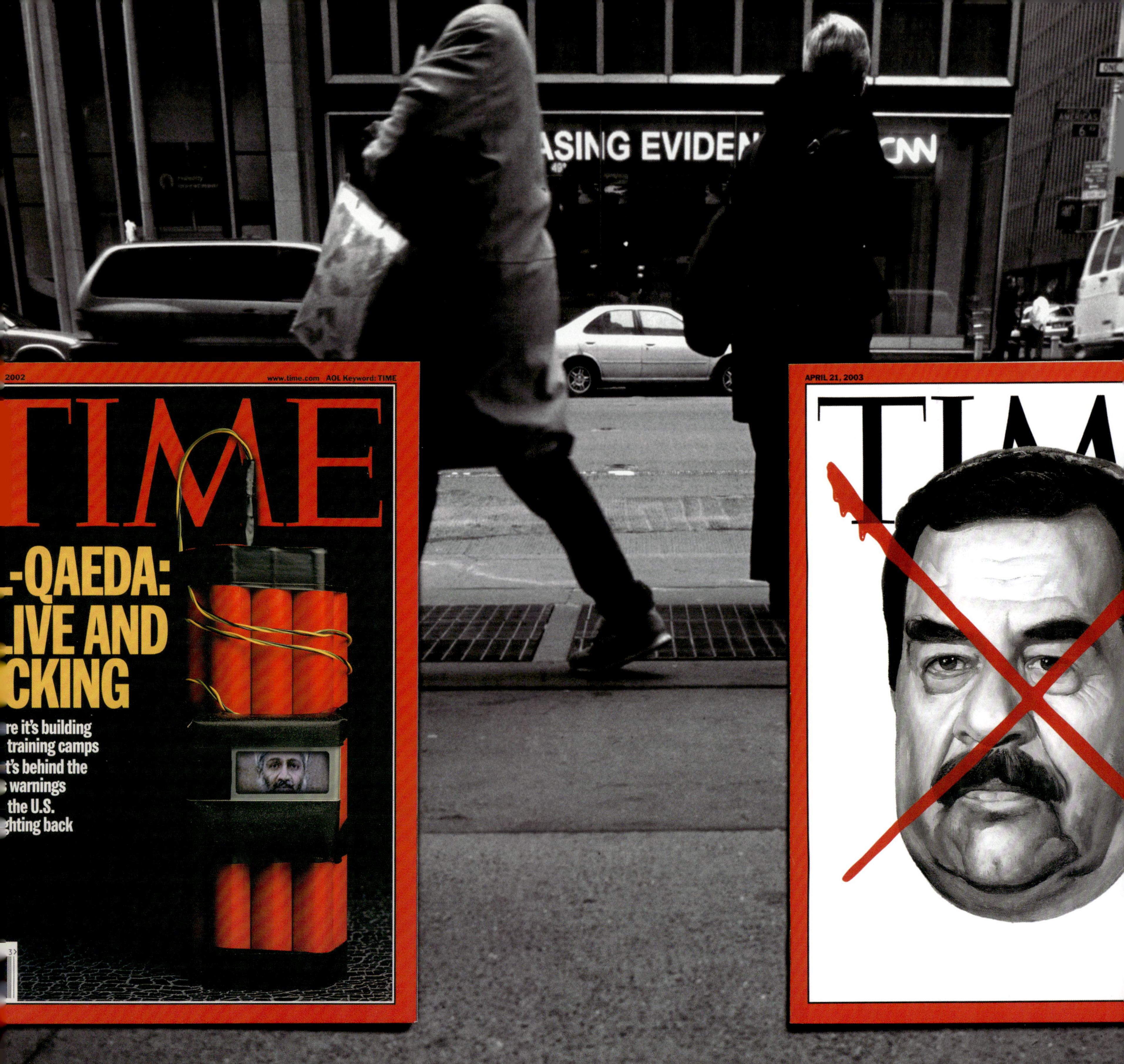
2002
www.time.com AOL Keyword: TIME
TIME
-QAEDA:
IVE AND
CKING
re it's building
training camps
t's behind the
warnings
the U.S.
ghting back
APRIL 21, 2003
TIM
ASING EVIDEN
CNN

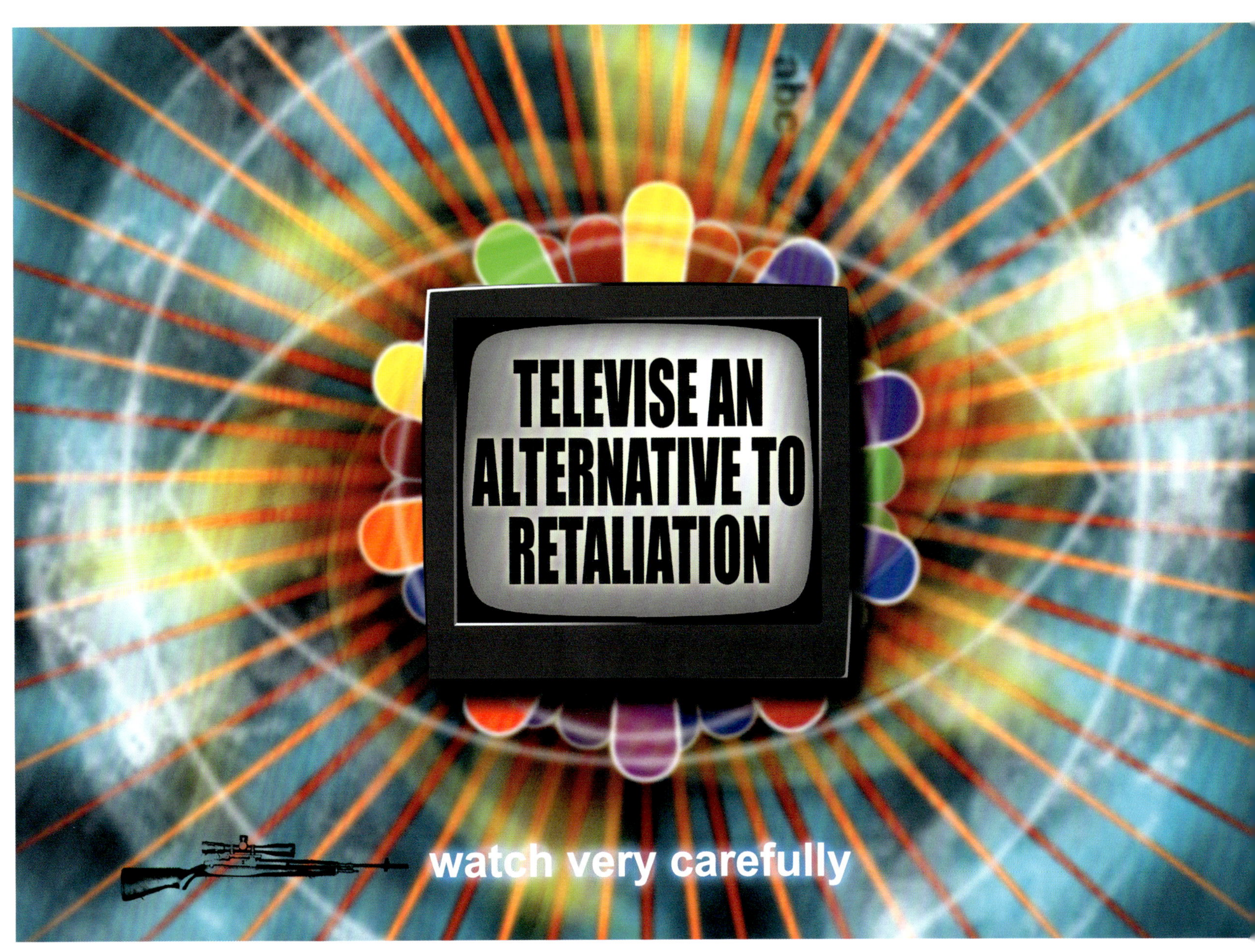

TELEVISE AN
ALTERNATIVE TO
RETALIATION
watch very carefully

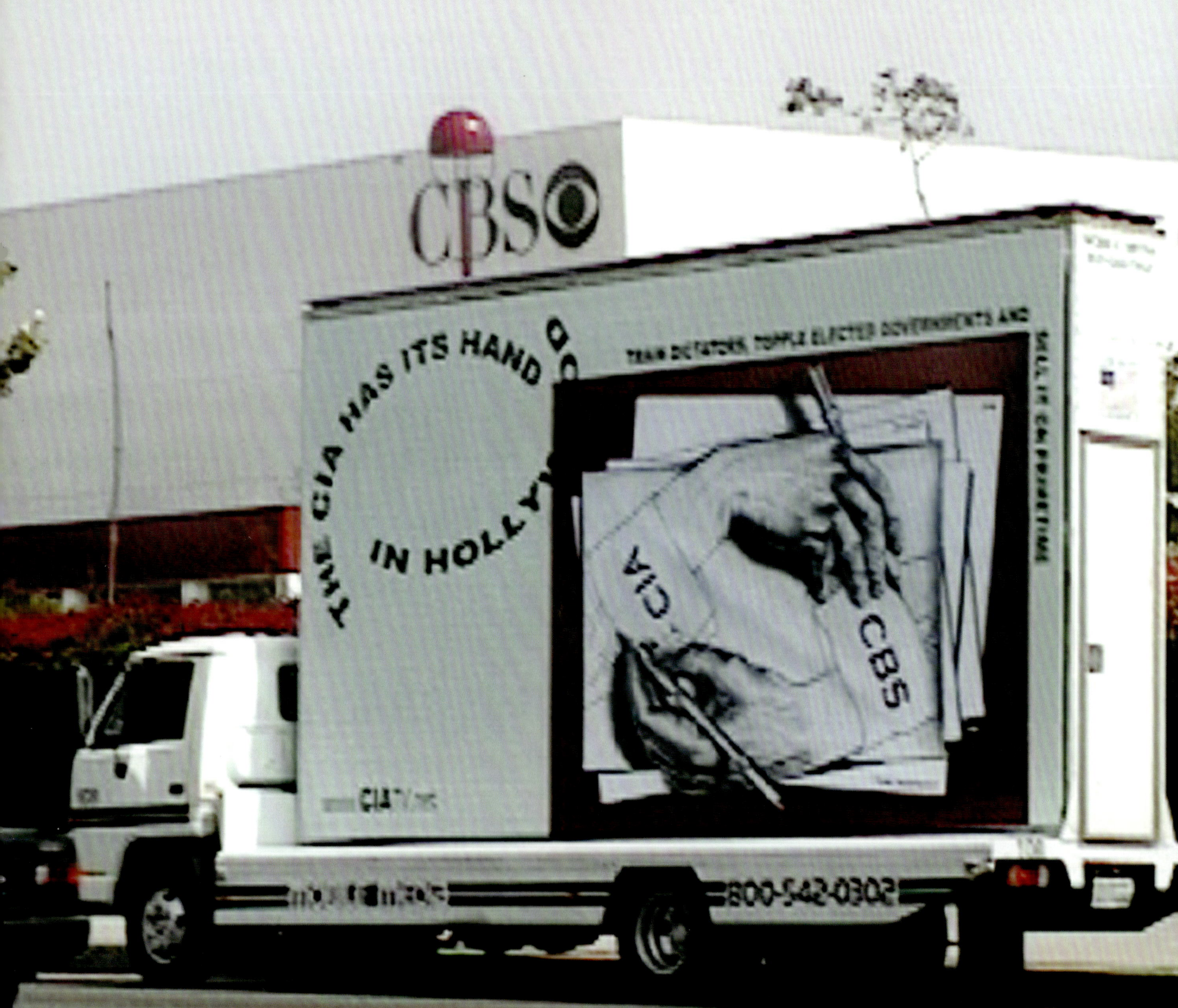

CBS
THE CIA HAS ITS HAND
IN HOLLYW
TRAIN DICTATORS, TOPPLE ELECTED GOVERNMENTS AND
CIA
CBS
CIA TV
800-542-0302

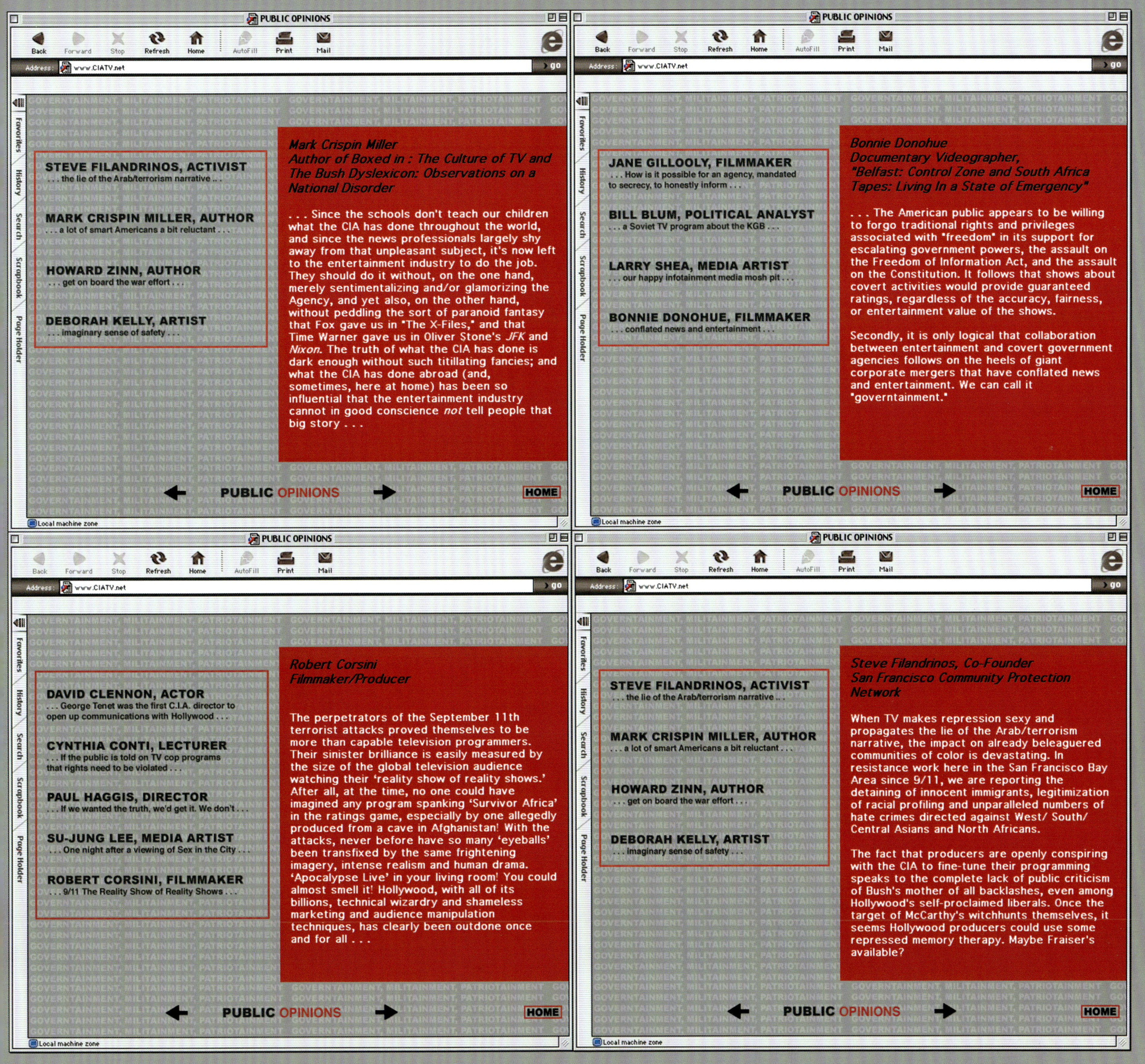

PUBLIC OPINIONS
Address: www.CIATV.net

STEVE FILANDRINOS, ACTIVIST
. . . the lie of the Arab/terrorism narrative . . .

MARK CRISPIN MILLER, AUTHOR
. . . a lot of smart Americans a bit reluctant . . .

HOWARD ZINN, AUTHOR
. . . get on board the war effort . . .

DEBORAH KELLY, ARTIST
. . . imaginary sense of safety . . .

Mark Crispin Miller
Author of Boxed in : The Culture of TV and The Bush Dyslexicon: Observations on a National Disorder

. . . Since the schools don't teach our children what the CIA has done throughout the world, and since the news professionals largely shy away from that unpleasant subject, it's now left to the entertainment industry to do the job. They should do it without, on the one hand, merely sentimentalizing and/or glamorizing the Agency, and yet also, on the other hand, without peddling the sort of paranoid fantasy that Fox gave us in "The X-Files," and that Time Warner gave us in Oliver Stone's JFK and Nixon. The truth of what the CIA has done is dark enough without such titillating fancies; and what the CIA has done abroad (and, sometimes, here at home) has been so influential that the entertainment industry cannot in good conscience not tell people that big story . . .

PUBLIC OPINIONS
HOME

PUBLIC OPINIONS
Address: www.CIATV.net

JANE GILLOOLY, FILMMAKER
. . . How is it possible for an agency, mandated to secrecy, to honestly inform . . .

BILL BLUM, POLITICAL ANALYST
. . . a Soviet TV program about the KGB . . .

LARRY SHEA, MEDIA ARTIST
. . . our happy infotainment media mosh pit . . .

BONNIE DONOHUE, FILMMAKER
. . . conflated news and entertainment . . .

Bonnie Donohue
Documentary Videographer,
"Belfast: Control Zone and South Africa Tapes: Living In a State of Emergency"

. . . The American public appears to be willing to forgo traditional rights and privileges associated with "freedom" in its support for escalating government powers, the assault on the Freedom of Information Act, and the assault on the Constitution. It follows that shows about covert activities would provide guaranteed ratings, regardless of the accuracy, fairness, or entertainment value of the shows.

Secondly, it is only logical that collaboration between entertainment and covert government agencies follows on the heels of giant corporate mergers that have conflated news and entertainment. We can call it "governtainment."

PUBLIC OPINIONS
HOME

PUBLIC OPINIONS
Address: www.CIATV.net

DAVID CLENNON, ACTOR
. . . George Tenet was the first C.I.A. director to open up communications with Hollywood . . .

CYNTHIA CONTI, LECTURER
. . . If the public is told on TV cop programs that rights need to be violated . . .

PAUL HAGGIS, DIRECTOR
. . . If we wanted the truth, we'd get it. We don't . . .

SU-JUNG LEE, MEDIA ARTIST
. . . One night after a viewing of Sex in the City . . .

ROBERT CORSINI, FILMMAKER
. . . 9/11 The Reality Show of Reality Shows . . .

Robert Corsini
Filmmaker/Producer

The perpetrators of the September 11th terrorist attacks proved themselves to be more than capable television programmers. Their sinister brilliance is easily measured by the size of the global television audience watching their 'reality show of reality shows.' After all, at the time, no one could have imagined any program spanking 'Survivor Africa' in the ratings game, especially by one allegedly produced from a cave in Afghanistan! With the attacks, never before have so many 'eyeballs' been transfixed by the same frightening imagery, intense realism and human drama. 'Apocalypse Live' in your living room! You could almost smell it! Hollywood, with all of its billions, technical wizardry and shameless marketing and audience manipulation techniques, has clearly been outdone once and for all . . .

PUBLIC OPINIONS
HOME

PUBLIC OPINIONS
Address: www.CIATV.net

STEVE FILANDRINOS, ACTIVIST
. . . the lie of the Arab/terrorism narrative . . .

MARK CRISPIN MILLER, AUTHOR
. . . a lot of smart Americans a bit reluctant . . .

HOWARD ZINN, AUTHOR
. . . get on board the war effort . . .

DEBORAH KELLY, ARTIST
. . . imaginary sense of safety . . .

Steve Filandrinos, Co-Founder
San Francisco Community Protection Network

When TV makes repression sexy and propagates the lie of the Arab/terrorism narrative, the impact on already beleaguered communities of color is devastating. In resistance work here in the San Francisco Bay Area since 9/11, we are reporting the detaining of innocent immigrants, legitimization of racial profiling and unparalleled numbers of hate crimes directed against West/ South/ Central Asians and North Africans.

The fact that producers are openly conspiring with the CIA to fine-tune their programming speaks to the complete lack of public criticism of Bush's mother of all backlashes, even among Hollywood's self-proclaimed liberals. Once the target of McCarthy's witchhunts themselves, it seems Hollywood producers could use some repressed memory therapy. Maybe Fraiser's available?

PUBLIC OPINIONS
HOME

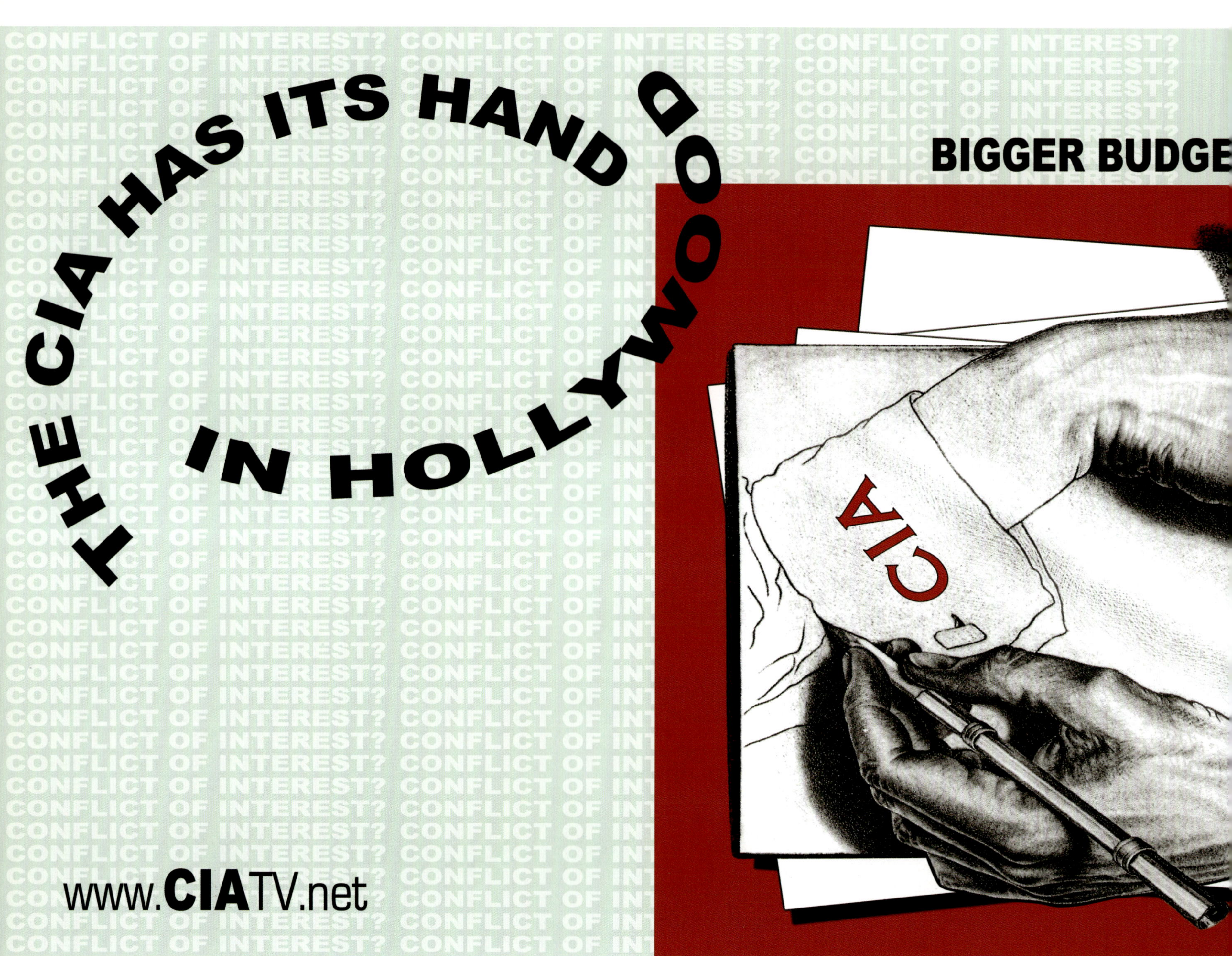

Preceding pages, Left: *CIA TV (Train Dictators, Topple Elected Governments, Sell It On Primetime)*, documentation of mobile billboard truck at Television City, Los Angeles, 2 Left: *CIA TV (Bigger Budgets, Higher Ratings, Now A Slot On Primetime)*, mobile billboard design, 10x20 ft, 2002. Right: Documentation of www.fox.com/24/research, 2003.

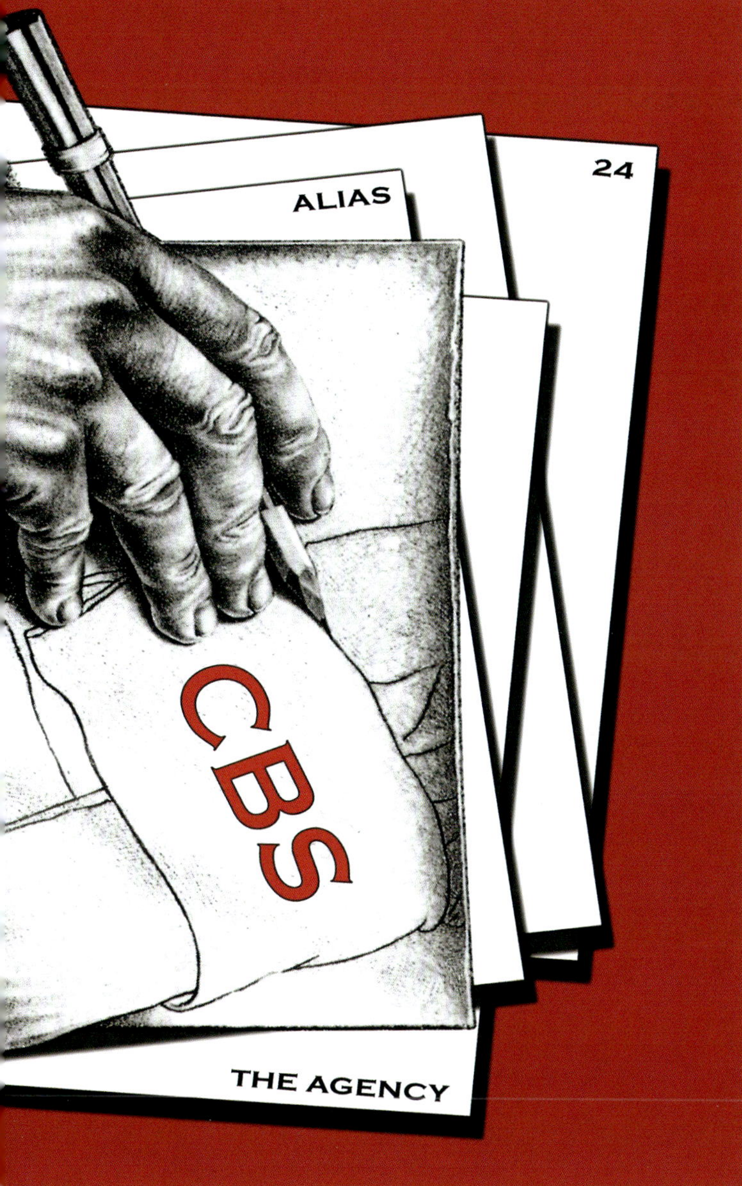

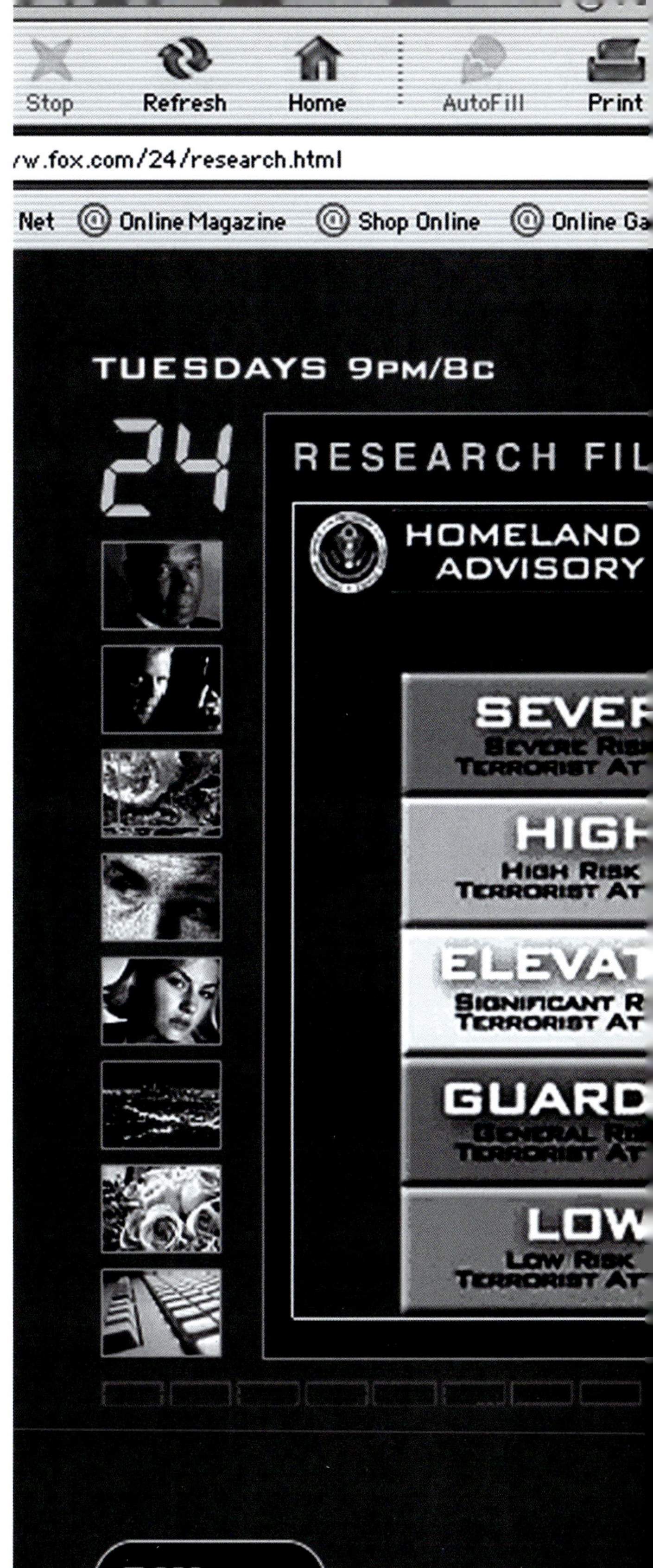

ight: *www.CIATV.net,* documentation of web resource, 2002.

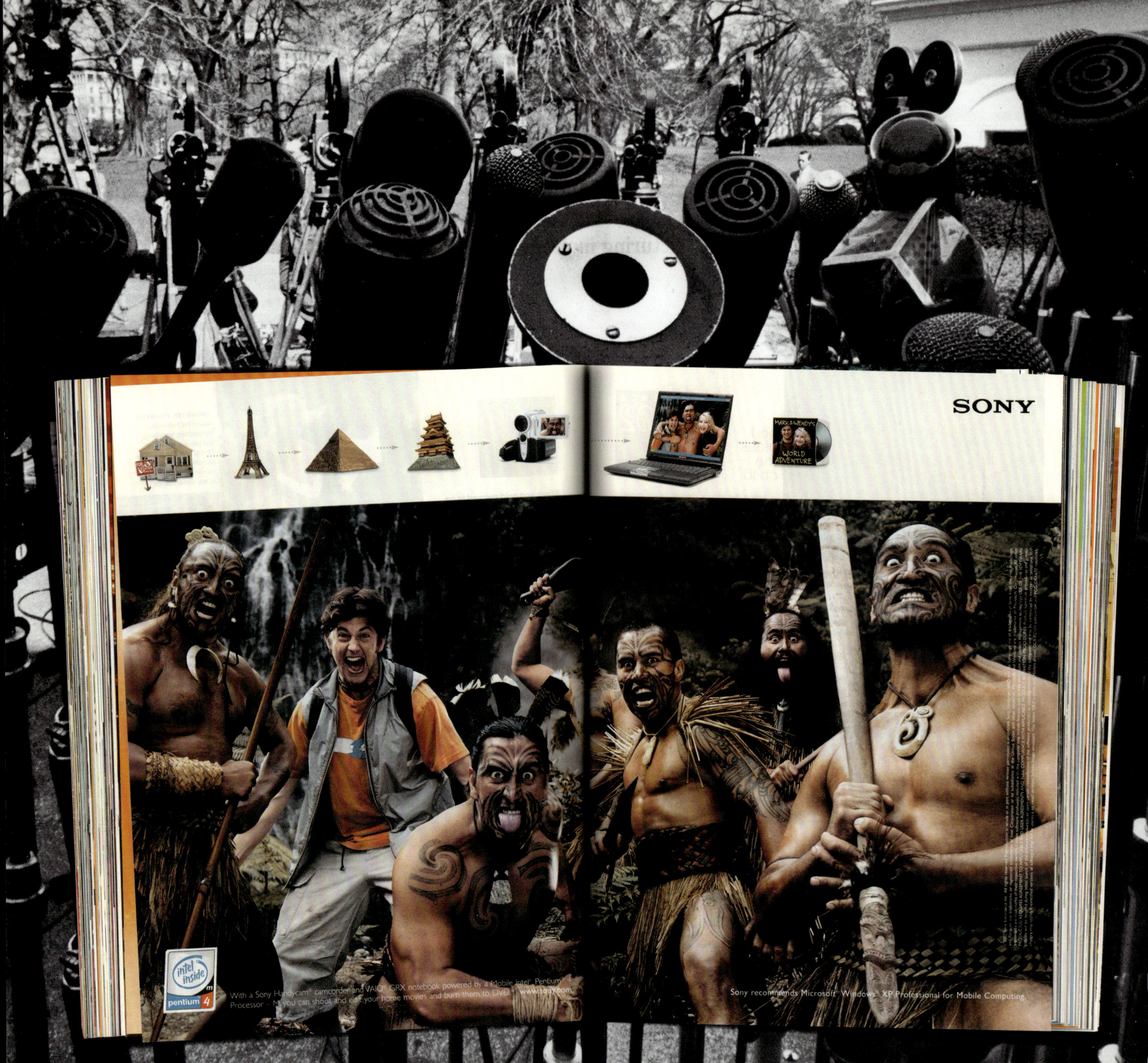

SONY
MARK & WENDY'S
WORLD ADVENTURE
intel inside m
pentium 4
With a Sony Handycam camcorder and VAIO GRX notebook powered by a Mobile Intel Pentium 4 Processor - M you can shoot and edit your home movies and burn them to DVD.
www.sony.com
Sony recommends Microsoft Windows XP Professional for Mobile Computing.

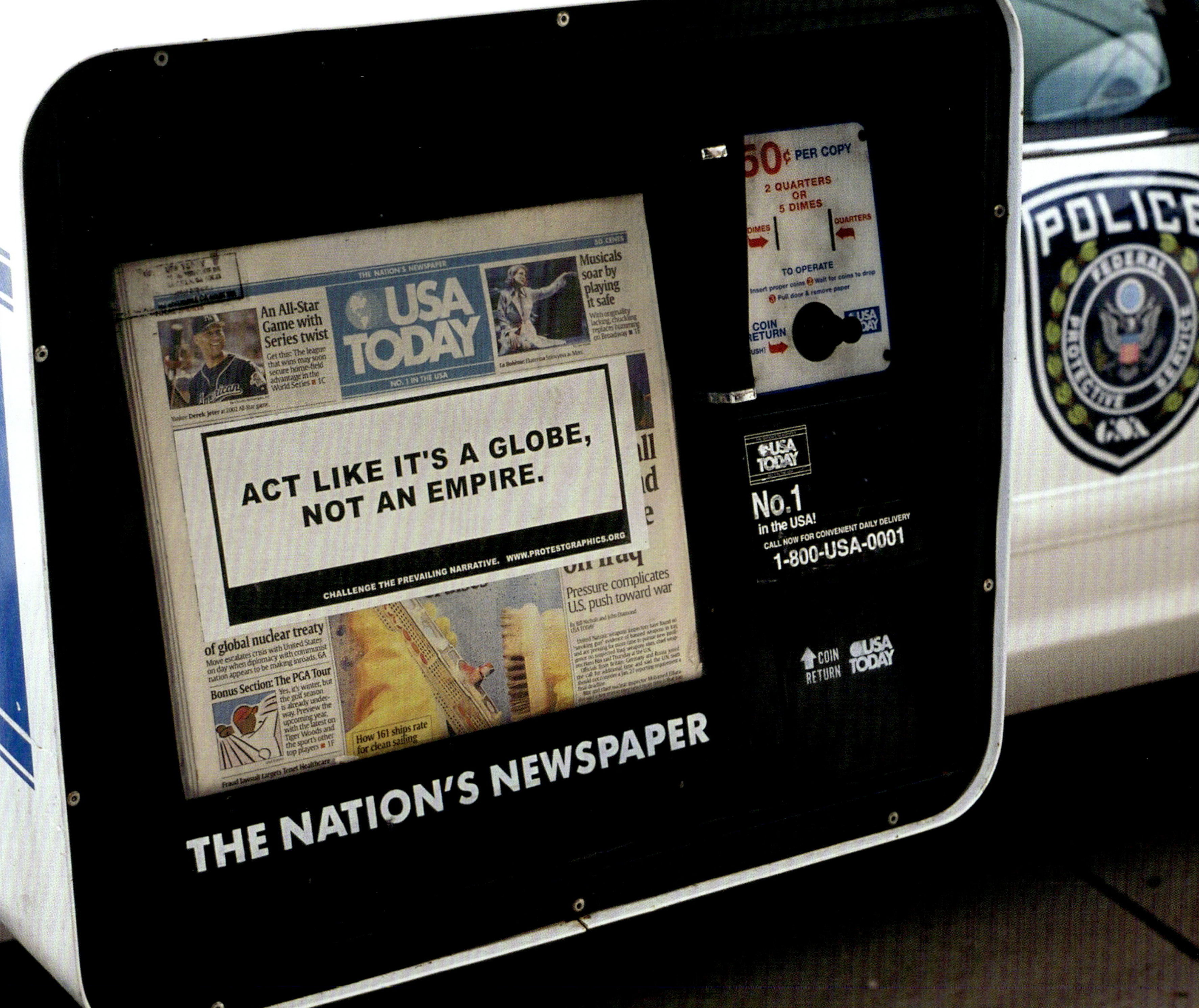

Left: *Sample #9 (Sony/Microphones Announcing US Non-Cooperation with (1) Convention on the Rights of the Child; (2) Convention on the Non-Applicability of Statutory Limitations to War Crimes and Crimes Against Humanity; (3) Second Optional Protocol to the International Covenant on Civil and Political Rights Aiming at the Abolition of the Death Penalty; (4) The Kyoto Protocol/Convention on Climate Change; (5) Rome Statute of the International Criminal Court; (6) Ottawa Treaty/Convention on the Prohibition of the Use, Stockpiling, Production, and Transfer of Anti-Personnel (Land)mines and on Their Destruction; (7) Comprehensive Nuclear-Test-Ban Treaty; (8) Convention on the Prohibition of the Development, Production, and Stockpiling of Bacteriological (Biological) and Toxin Weapons and on Their Destruction; (9) International Convention Against the Recruitment, Use, Financing, and Training of Mercenaries; among others)*, collage, dimensions variable, 2003. Right: *Act Like It's A Globe, Not An Empire*, newspaper stand intervention, 2003.

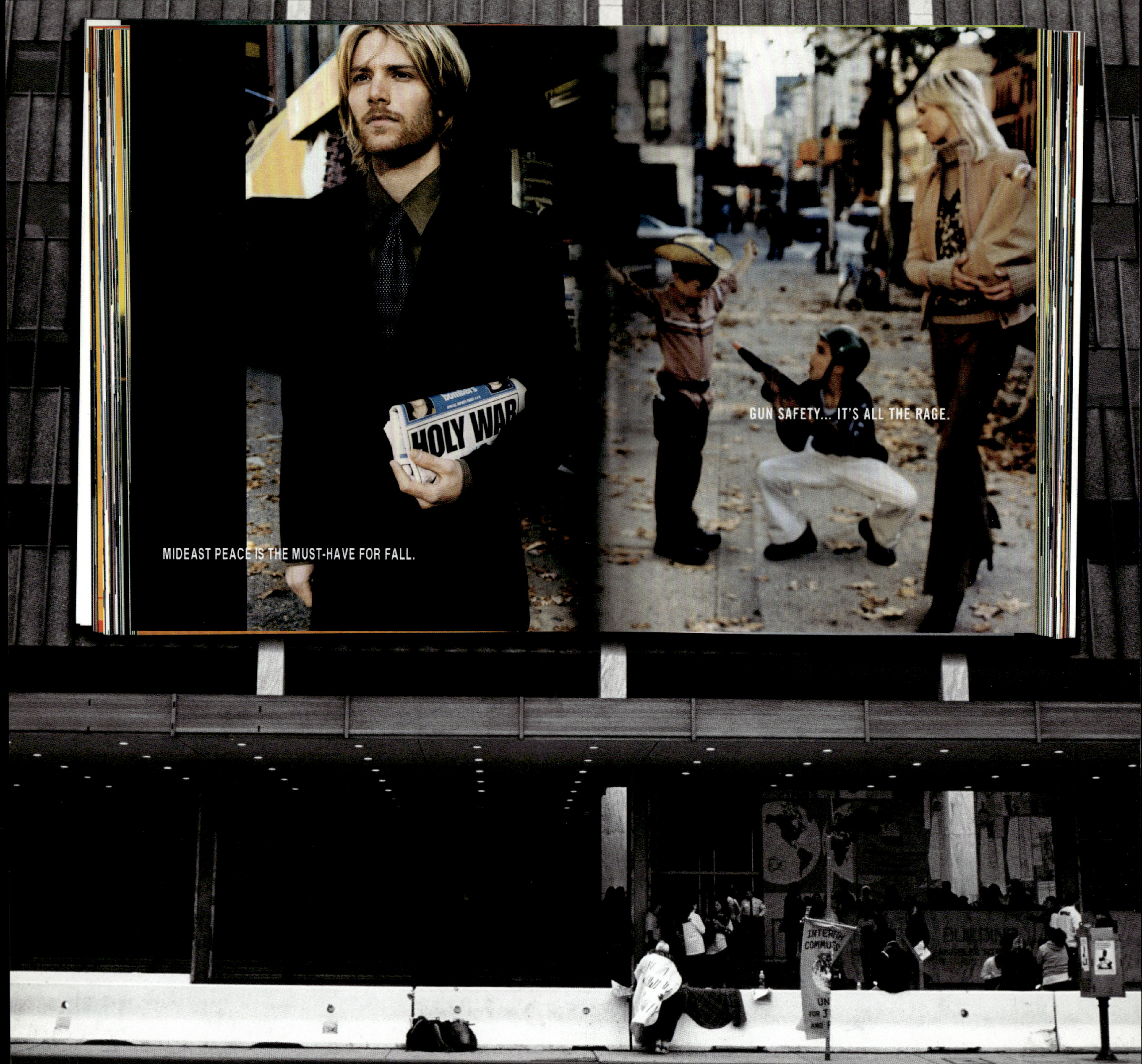

HOLY WAR
MIDEAST PEACE IS THE MUST-HAVE FOR FALL.
GUN SAFETY... IT'S ALL THE RAGE.

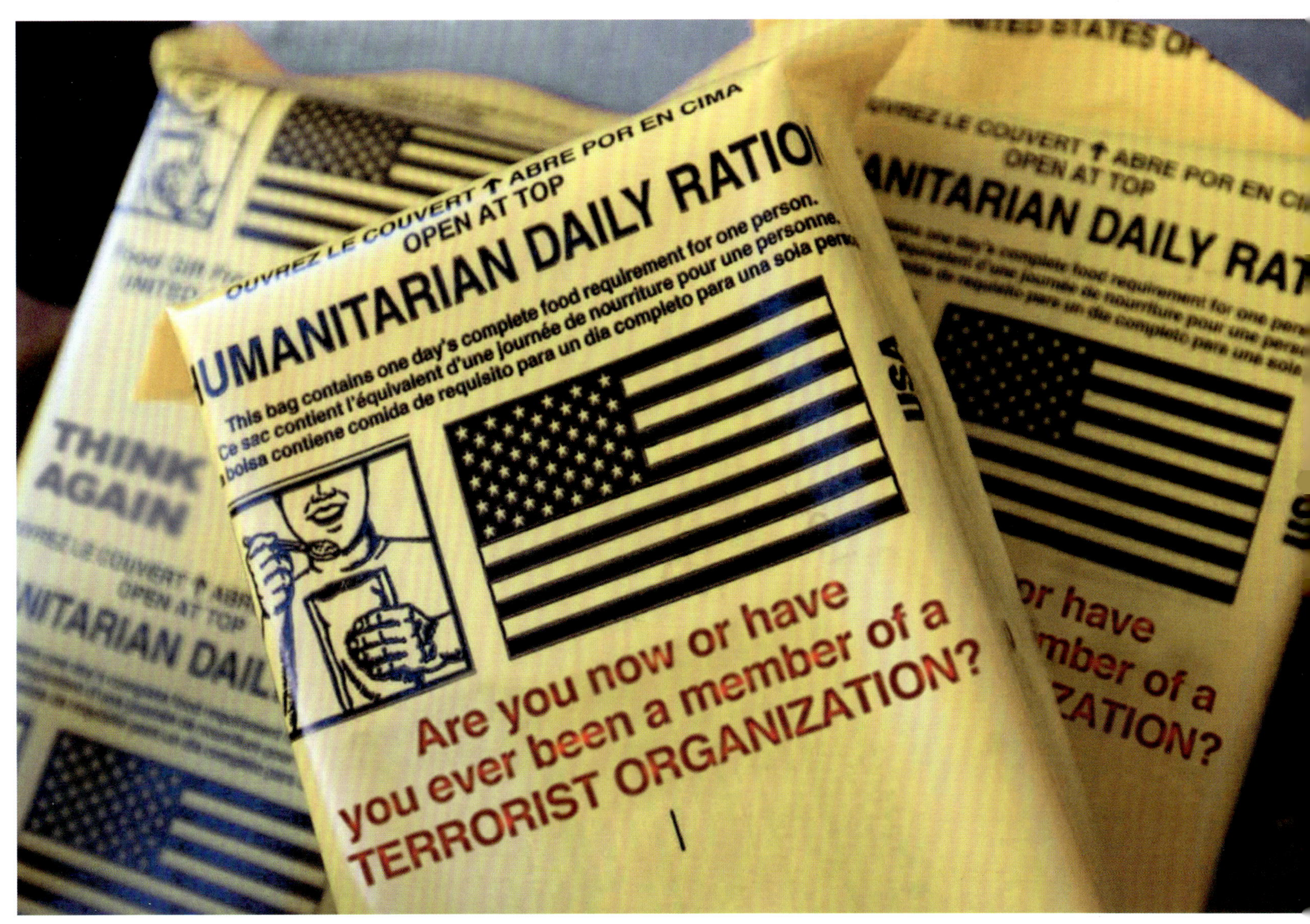

Left: *Sample #10 (Kenneth Cole/Kenneth Cole/Los Angeles INS Headquarters During "Voluntary" Registration of Males from Afghanistan, Algeria, Bahrain, Eritrea, Lebanon, Morocco, North Korea, Oman, Qatar, Somalia, Tunisia, The United Arab Emirates, and Yemen with Pending US Green Card Applications)*, collage, dimensions variable, 2003. Right: *Humanitarian Daily Ration*, digital poster, dimensions variable, 2001.

KEN MARTIN—IMPACT DIGITALS

J'ACCUSE, 2001: Where have you gone, Emile Zola?

IT'S ALL OUR FAULT

Shades of the '60s: Academic radicals form the core of an angry, reactionary and increasingly irrelevant force—American anti-Americanism. **BY ALAN WOLFE**

THE SEPTEMBER 11 attacks "niggerized" America. Mayor Rudolph Giuliani of New York City is "known for his virulently Zionist views." Terms such as "international terrorism" are useless in explaining why innocent lives were lost. The responses of American politicians and media commentators amount to "self-righteous drivel and outright deceptions." If you did not know these things, you have not been following the views of, respectively, Cornel West, Edward Said, Stanley Fish and Susan Sontag.

The 1960s burn brightly for some of America's most distinguished literary critics and theorists—and nothing will extinguish the flame. To them, the United States is a bully that deploys its corporate and military power to crush opponents, and Americans are racists or craven dummies misled by the propaganda of complicit media. Only intellectuals like themselves who dare speak truth to power can save the world from American arrogance.

A reactionary is someone determined to hang on to the past at all costs. By that standard the academic left, if these writers and thinkers are representative, is becoming one of the most reactionary forces in America. Susan Sontag finds a way to blame "specific American alliances and actions" for the deaths of innocents on September 11. It doesn't matter that the perpetrators were Middle Eastern

---

RFC No.	642806	Los Angeles Poli[ce] NOTICE TO

BOOKING NO. (JAIN ★) 763074
DATE AND TIME RELEASED O.R. ★   DR. LIC. NO. ★
MARCH 21, 2003   3-21-03   2330 HRS   101618114

LAST NAME, FIRST, MIDDLE ★
RAHMAN, SHELLEY

RESIDENCE ADDRESS ★   CITY   STATE
15185 WARING AV   LA   CA
BUSINESS ADDRESS ★   CITY   STATE

SEX ★ | DESC ★ | HAIR ★ | EYES ★ | HEIGHT ★ | WEIGHT ★ | D.O.B. ★
F | WHT | BRN | BRN | 509 | 135 | 1-4-

MISC. DESCRIPTIVE INFORMATION (SCARS, TATTOOS, ETC.) ★
TT ON LT ARM (DESIGN)

VEH. LIC. NO. ★ | YR. | VEH. YR. | MAKE ★
40A 244 | 03 | 93 | JEEP

R.D. ★ | DIV. & DETAIL ARREST ★ | DATE & TIME OF ARREST
645 | HWD - 6W50 | MARCH 21, 20

REGISTERED OWNER ★
PASS
REGISTERED OWNER'S ADDRESS ★   CITY   STATE
PASS

VIOLATIONS (SECTION NO. & CODE) ★
1- 28.04 (A) LAMC   2-   3-
DESCRIPTION OF VIOLATION ★
1. POSTING SIGNS ONTO CITY PROP[ERTY]

APPROX. SPEED | PF/MAX. SPEED | VEH. SPEED LIMIT
0 | 75 | —

LOCATION OF VIOLATION(S) - IN CITY OF LOS ANGELES, ON ★
ORANGE DR - LANEWOOD

☑ OFFENSE(S) NOT COMMITTED IN MY PRESENCE. CERTIFIED ON INFORMATION AN[D]
I CERTIFY UNDER PENALTY OF PERJURY THAT THE FOREGOING IS TRUE AND C[ORRECT]
EXECUTED ON THE DATE SHOWN ABOVE AT LOS ANGELES, CALIF.

ISSUING OFFICER ★   SERIAL NO.   UNAVAILABLE DATES
TM   34404   PAS[S]

ARRESTING OFCR. IF DIFFERENT THAN ABOVE-SER. NO. ★   UNAVAILABLE
RUSSELL   25670   PA[SS]

WITHOUT ADMITTING GUILT, I PROMISE TO APPEAR AS INDICATED
SIN DECLARARME CULPABLE, PROMETO APARECER TAL COMO IND[ICATED]
SIGNATURE
FIRMA   X

✓	LOCATION TO APPEAR		DATE
DIV. 61	1945 S. HILL ST., L.A.		
DIV.			
COURT CLERK ROOM 210	429 BAUCHET ST., L.A.		
DIV. 85	505 S. CENTRE ST., SAN PEDRO		
COURT CLERK ROOM 202			
DIV. 90	1633 PURDUE AVE., W.L.A.		
COURT CLERK ROOM 101			
DIV. 97	11701 S. LA CIENEGA BLVD., L.A.		
MUNICIPAL COURT CLERK			
DIV. 101	14400 ERWIN ST. MALL VAN NUYS		
COURT CLERK ROOM 200			
DIV. 130	900 3RD ST., SAN FERNANDO		
MUNICIPAL COURT CLERK			
COURT CLERK ROOM 102	5925 HOLLYWOOD BLVD., HOLLYWOOD		APRIL 18, 2003
DIV.			

FORM APPROVED BY THE JUDICIAL COUNCIL OF CALIFORNIA(S) 12[...]
V.C. 40500(B), 40513(B), & 40522, P.C. 853.9
70-05.02.02 (10/00)
— SEE REVERSE —

Left: *Sample #11 (City of Hollywood Arrest Citation for Posting Protestgraphics/Newsweek International Edition with Illustration of Protestgraphics),* collage, dimensions variable, 2003. Right: *Bitter Pill,* digital poster, dimensions variable, 2001.

Following pages
Left: Documentation of *Protestgraphics*, Boston, 2001. Right: Documentation of *Protestgraphics*, Los Angeles, 2003.

Following pages
Right: Documentation of THINK AGAIN distributing materials at anti-war demonstration, Los Angeles, 2003. Right: Documentation of THINK AGAIN distributing postcards at Pride Parade, Boston, 1999.

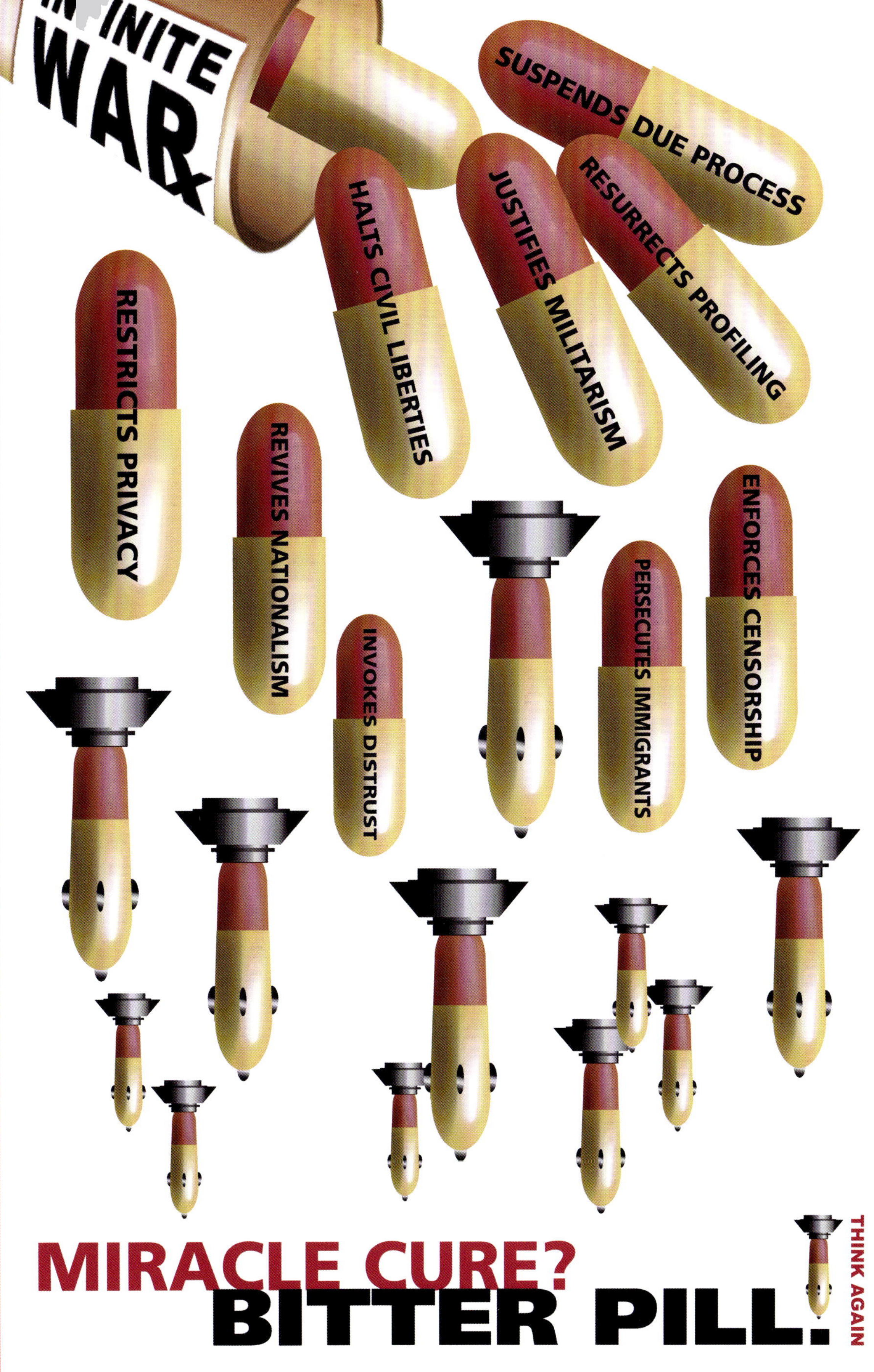

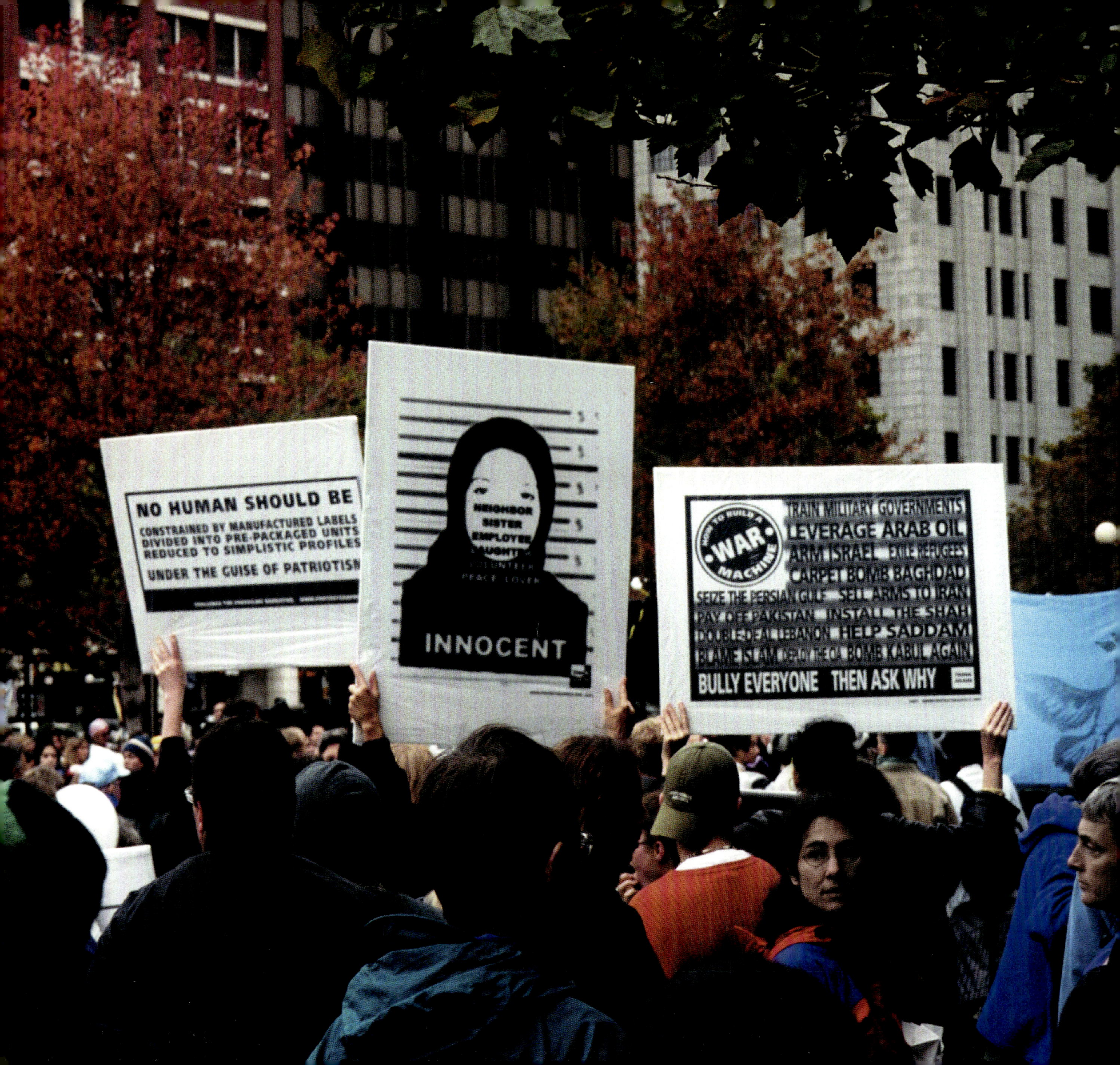

NO HUMAN SHOULD BE
CONSTRAINED BY MANUFACTURED LABELS
DIVIDED INTO PRE-PACKAGED UNITS
REDUCED TO SIMPLISTIC PROFILES
UNDER THE GUISE OF PATRIOTISM

NEIGHBOR
SISTER
EMPLOYEE
DAUGHTER
VOLUNTEER
PEACE LOVER
INNOCENT

HOW TO BUILD A
WAR
MACHINE
TRAIN MILITARY GOVERNMENTS
LEVERAGE ARAB OIL
ARM ISRAEL   EXILE REFUGEES
CARPET BOMB BAGHDAD
SEIZE THE PERSIAN GULF   SELL ARMS TO IRAN
PAY OFF PAKISTAN   INSTALL THE SHAH
DOUBLE-DEAL LEBANON   HELP SADDAM
BLAME ISLAM   DEPLOY THE CIA   BOMB KABUL AGAIN
BULLY EVERYONE   THEN ASK WHY

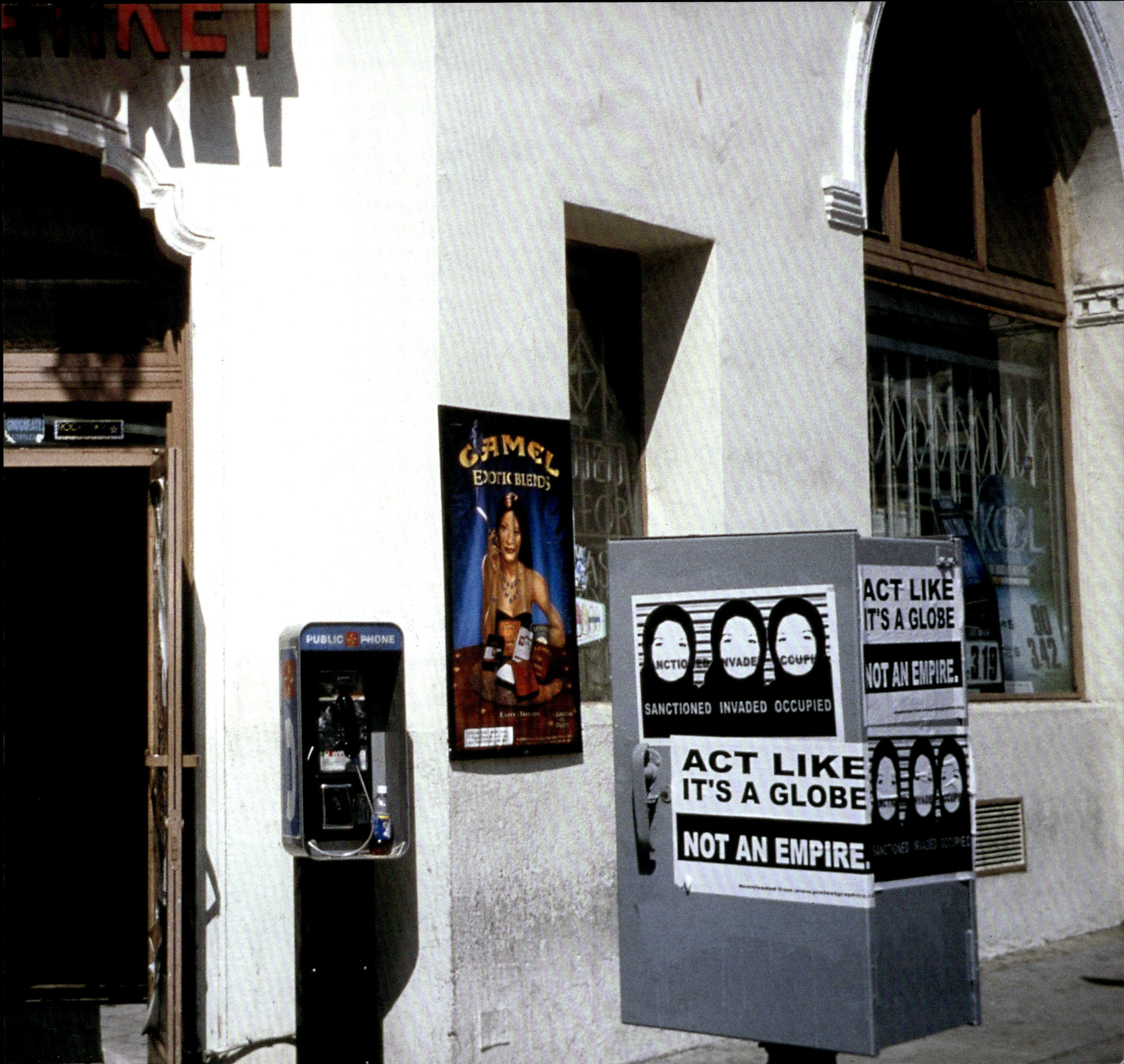
MARKET
PUBLIC PHONE
CAMEL
EXOTIC BLENDS
SANCTIONED INVADED OCCUPIED
ACT LIKE
IT'S A GLOBE
NOT AN EMPIRE.
ACT LIKE
IT'S A GLOBE
NOT AN EMPIRE.
SANCTIONED INVADED OCCUPIED

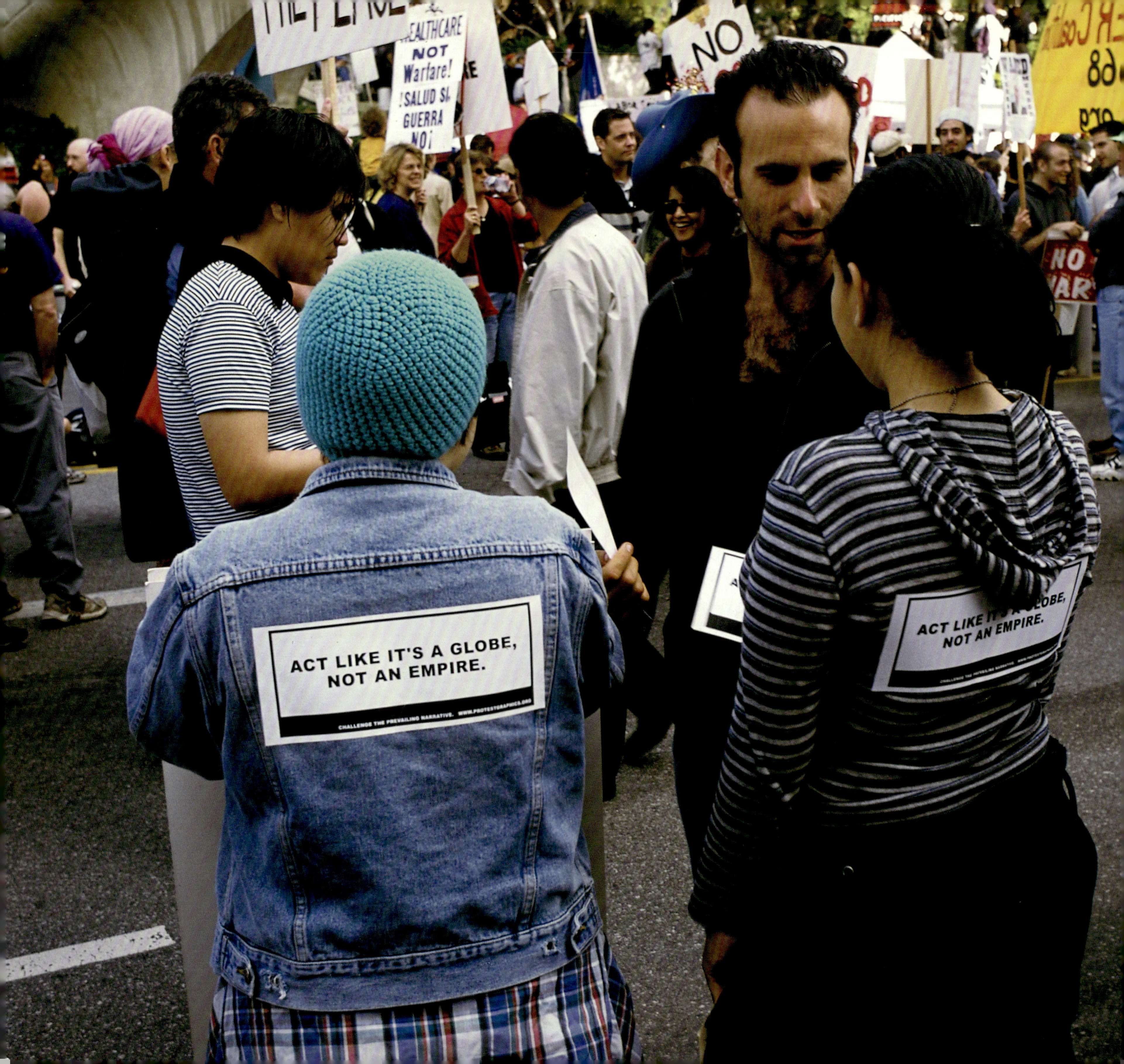

ACT LIKE IT'S A GLOBE,
NOT AN EMPIRE.
ACT LIKE IT'S A GLOBE,
NOT AN EMPIRE.
HEALTHCARE
NOT
Warfare!
!SALUD SI,
GUERRA
NO!
NO WAR

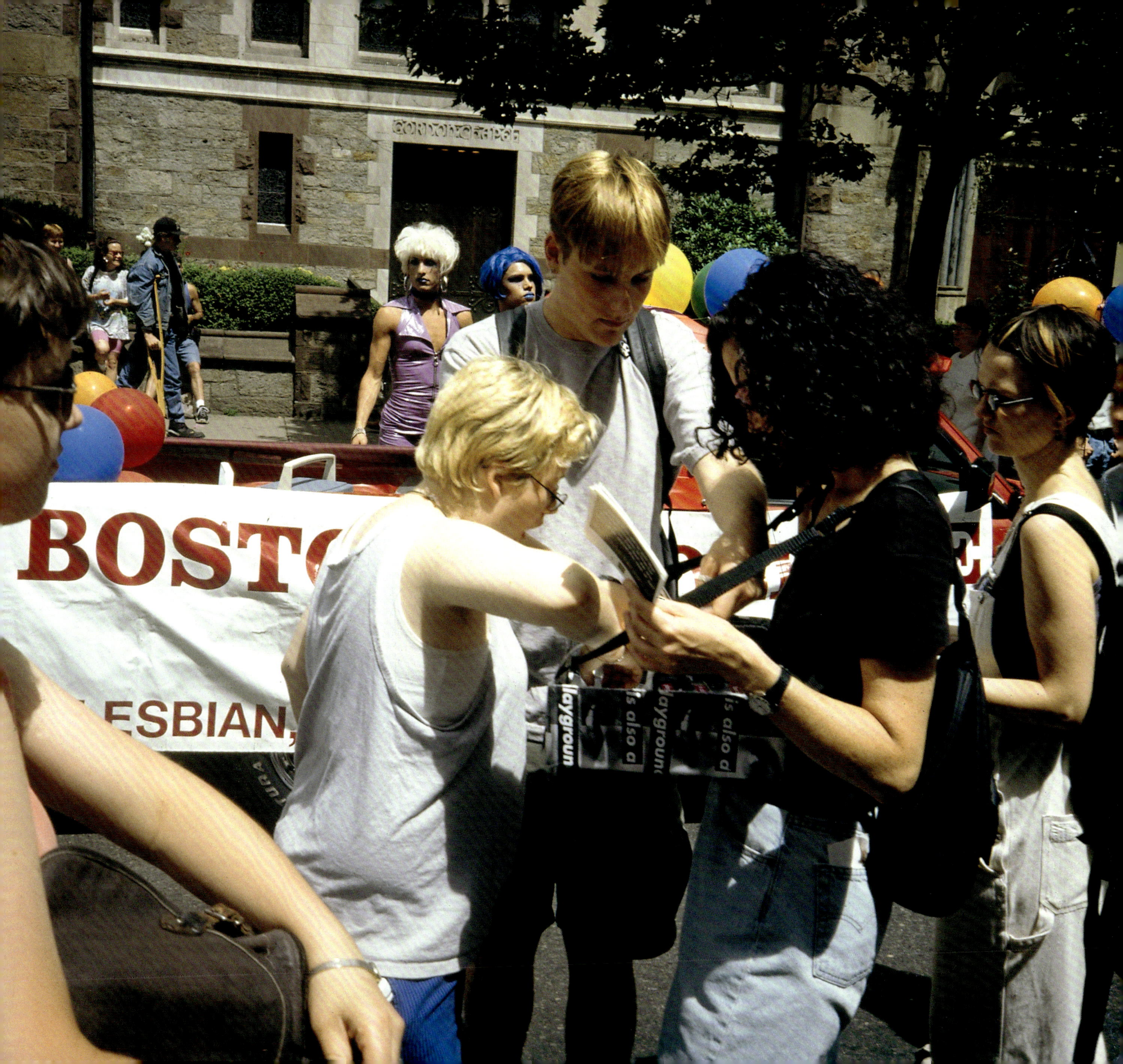
BOSTO
ESBIAN,

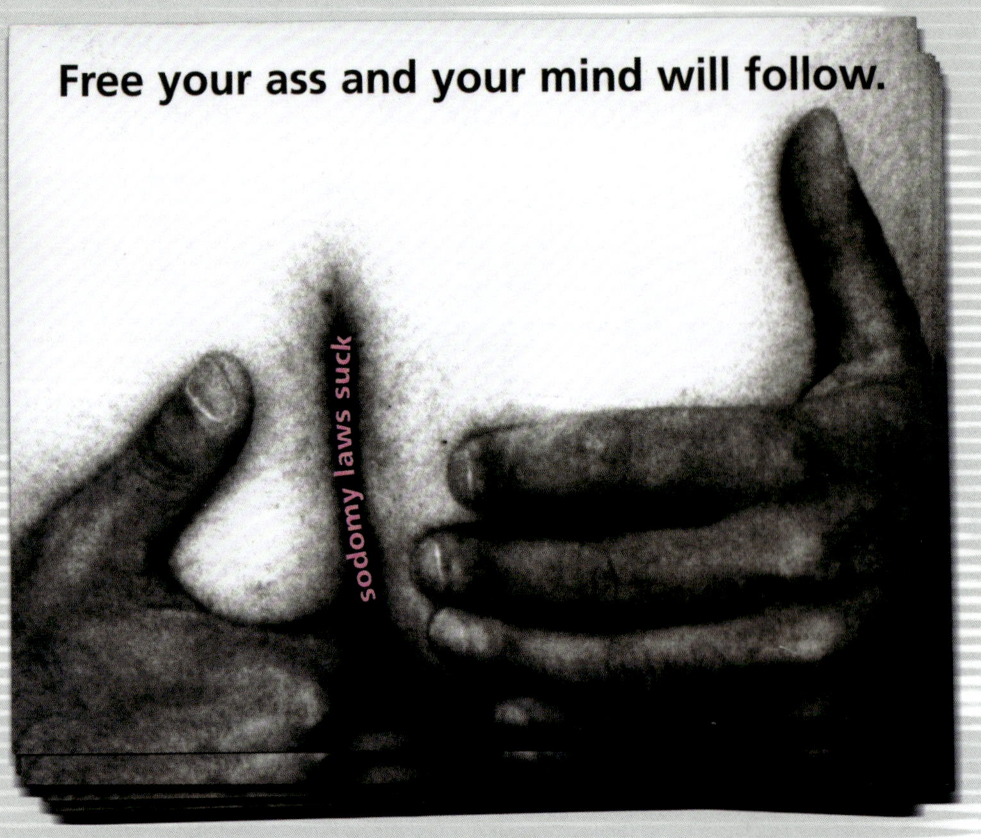

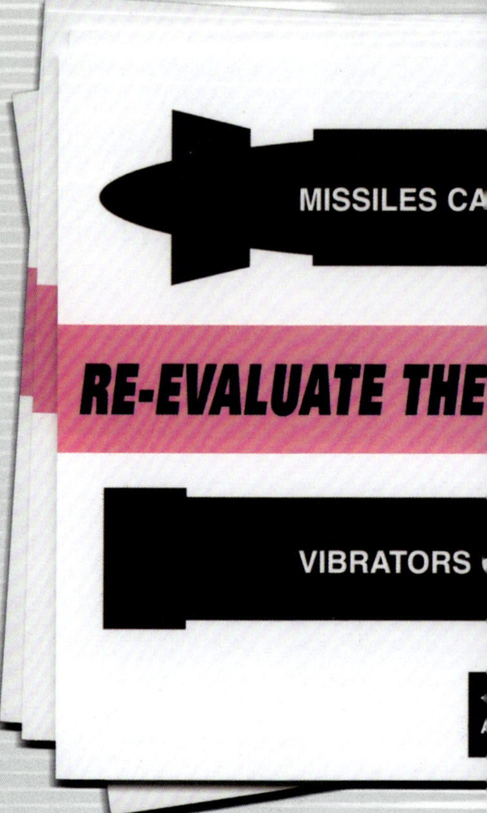

Nineteen states have laws criminalizing
consensual sex between adults.
Sexual freedom is a civil right.

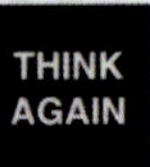

MAKE NOISE NOT WAR.